Mixed-Ability Teaching

Mixed-Ability Teaching

Edmund Dudley and Erika Osváth

OXFORD
UNIVERSITY PRESS

Great Clarendon Street, Oxford, OX2 6DP, United Kingdom

Oxford University Press is a department of the University of Oxford.
It furthers the University's objective of excellence in research, scholarship,
and education by publishing worldwide. Oxford is a registered trade
mark of Oxford University Press in the UK and in certain other countries

© Oxford University Press 2016

The moral rights of the author have been asserted

First published in 2016

2024

10 9 8 7

No unauthorized photocopying

Links to third party websites are provided by Oxford in good faith and for
information only. Oxford disclaims any responsibility for the materials
contained in any third party website referenced in this work

ISBN: 978 0 19 420038 7

Printed in Great Britain by Ashford Colour Press Ltd.

This book is printed on paper from certified and well-managed sources

ACKNOWLEDGEMENTS

Sources: p.20 "J. K. Rowling", https://simple.wikipedia.org, accessed
17 September 2015. p.21 English Plus: Student's Book 1 by Ben Wetz and
Diana Pye (Oxford University Press, 2010).

Back cover photograph: Oxford University Press building/David Fisher

Acknowledgements

We would like to thank Andrew Dilger for his brilliant editorial guidance, expert insights and feedback.

The ideas and activities featured in this book have emerged slowly over many years in the classroom. Ed owes a debt of gratitude (and perhaps an apology or two) to all the students who have passed through his classroom doors over the years. There were plenty of rotten activities along the way, which only they had to endure. He would also like to thank the English teachers at PTE Babits Mihály Secondary School in Pécs, Hungary, for many years of friendship, support and inspiration. Special thanks go to his incredible daughters, Réka and Dóra, the wisest and funniest teenage advisers. Of. All. Time.

Erika would like to thank her mother Ilona and her father Imre, whose lessons as primary school teachers opened up a world of wonder and inspiration. Her heartfelt thanks go to her students over the years who, through their uniqueness, have made her think about all the many different ways to teach. She would also like to express her gratitude to her colleagues: stimulating discussions with them brought about revealing insights into how the ideas in this book can work in different teaching contexts. Finally, a special word of thanks to her lovely daughters Alma and Kamilla for always being ready to try out ideas and give her feedback on how they work, and for being incredibly patient with her during the writing process. Like Réka and Dóra, they are also the wisest young advisers in this part of the world.

Contents

Introduction

Every block of stone has a statue inside it and it is the task of the sculptor to discover it.
MICHELANGELO

Who this book is for

This book is for teachers working with mixed-ability English-language groups. The prospect of teaching students of different levels can be daunting if you have relatively little classroom experience; at the same time, teachers with lots of experience under their belt might also be looking for strategies and techniques to help them get the best out of their mixed-ability groups. Whatever your own situation, the practical activities that this book contains can be adapted and tried out in your own classroom.

To some degree, all classes are mixed-ability. The 'blocks of stone' may all appear to be similar, but each one has its own unique potential and characteristics. As teachers, our job is to familiarize ourselves with the 'raw materials' with which we are working. It is only by becoming aware of students' needs, strengths, and capabilities that we can identify the right tools with which to work. Successful mixed-ability teaching is therefore not about 'forming' students to match a template in our minds, but about enabling their own potential to be discovered and realized.

When we think about the different students that we teach, one of the first things we think about is language level. In a mixed-ability class, there is a significant difference in language proficiency between individual students. This alone creates a special set of challenges for the teacher. Although we refer to 'stronger' and 'weaker' students throughout the book, this is purely a description of linguistic ability. The knowledge that all individual students have a range of non-linguistic strengths that can and should be recognized is at the heart of the approach to mixed-ability teaching presented in this book.

Teachers have a decisive role to play in harnessing the potential of mixed-ability groups. Careful preparation, selection, and differentiation of activities can make language more accessible to learners. The way we plan classes and the decisions we take during lessons can go a long way to making sure that different students in a mixed-ability group are kept involved and motivated. We also need to be aware of our words and actions, remembering that effective communication means talking to different students in different ways. The way we speak to individual students and the feedback we give can have a huge impact on their attitudes to learning, and this is another important aspect of successful mixed-ability teaching.

The most important goal for a teacher is to help students become the best that <u>they</u> can be. For that we need an individualized approach to teaching and learning, complete with personalized outcomes that can differ from student to student.

We hope that this book will provide teachers with practical tools for discovering and freeing the potential of their own mixed-ability groups.

A word of reassurance

Most strategies that work with mixed-ability classes are simply good teaching strategies, and you probably know many of them already. You do not need to develop a whole new way of teaching, but you might need to apply your strategies more consistently and consciously to bring about a learning environment in which all of your students can make real progress.

How this book is organized

In Part 1 we will look at how we can best prepare for a mixed-ability group, including ways to find out about your learners and plan **differentiated** activities. Managing the classroom effectively is another important feature of successful mixed-ability teaching, and that is what we will focus on in Part 2. If you teach in a monolingual setting and share the native language of your students, then the ideas offered in Part 3 might suggest ways in which the students' native language can stimulate learning in your mixed-ability groups. Introducing new language and developing the four skills is a key component of English teaching – but how can it best be done in a mixed-ability setting? This is the question that we will address in Part 4. Although mixed groups present plenty of challenges for the teacher, in Parts 5 and 6 we will discuss the ways in which the differences between learners can add variety and value to our lessons, especially if we are able to introduce collaborative and cooperative working modes that energize and engage our students. In Part 7 we look at the options available for teachers who are interested in assessing their learners in ways that acknowledge individual learning needs and capabilities, perhaps in conjunction with more traditional forms of assessment. Finally, in Part 8 we will look at mixed-ability teaching in the broader context of interpersonal interaction, and at ways that recognizing and acknowledging the attitudes, emotions, and personalities of our students can lead to higher levels of motivation and a more harmonious classroom environment for everyone.

Although there are many links between the chapters in the book, you do not need to read it from beginning to end. Each chapter can be read on its own, and the ideas presented will give you tools and techniques that can be used with mixed-ability classrooms covering various teaching areas.

The main text of the book deals with the pedagogy behind each topic discussed within the mixed-ability context. *Try this* activities provide you with specific ideas and techniques that you can try immediately. *Getting it right* sections give procedural tips for some of the more specific suggestions. *Why this works* sections provide a pedagogic rationale for activities where important and helpful. In addition, there is a *Glossary* for words that appear in bold throughout the main text, a list of *Useful websites* for extending or developing activities online, and a list of *Frequently asked questions* which refer you to specific pages of the book itself to find the answers.

Part 1

Preparing for a mixed-ability class

1   Identifying variables

A teacher's job is not only to teach the language – it is also to help learners engage with it. In order to know what kind of language to teach and how to teach it, we need to know something about the students we will be working with. By exploring the variables within and between learners in a mixed-ability group, teachers not only gain insights into the best way of approaching individuals within the group, but also begin to develop a sense of the defining features of the class as a whole.

Collecting data

A number of factors combine to give each class its own unique profile. The language level of students is a key variable, but it is by no means the only important criterion. Placement tests will provide information about students' language level, but the needs, attitudes, and personalities of the students also need to be explored. Questions to consider include:

- Why are the students learning English?
- What specifically do they need to learn?
- What is their attitude towards learning the language?
- How do they feel about being a member of this group?
- What are their interests outside school?

In certain cases, the teacher might already know the answers to some of these questions. Rather than making assumptions, it makes sense to ask the students themselves. Questionnaires, surveys, and specially prepared worksheets are particularly useful data collection tools for this purpose in the mixed-ability classroom. They can provide the basis for classroom activities that not only give us the information we need, but also offer natural opportunities for language practice. In addition, they enable teachers to send a clear message that they are interested in students' needs and preferences.

Questionnaires, surveys, and worksheets

Questionnaires designed by the teacher can be used to gather data about students' preferences regarding learning methods, topics, classroom activities, and types of input. We can also design activities so that students provide information about themselves: their personality, interests, and ambitions. A key benefit of doing this is that it helps students to think about different aspects of language learning and encourages them to prioritize their own needs. By guiding them to focus on their own learning, we can help them to become aware of their own responsibilities.

Try this ☞ **Questionnaire about learning**

Design a simple questionnaire about learning English for the class. See the example below. The focus of the questionnaire should not be limited to aspects of language but can also include questions about learning methods and ways of working in class. Statements a–g provide a few examples of areas that can be addressed when creating questionnaires for mixed-ability groups. Discuss the questionnaire with the class afterwards.

> **Score each sentence on a scale of 1–5.**
> **(1 = I disagree strongly, 5 = I agree strongly)**
> a) I need to do more grammar practice activities.   _____
> b) I would like to read more in English.   _____
> c) I enjoy speaking activities in class.   _____
> d) I need to improve my pronunciation.   _____
> e) I think it is important to use technology in the classroom.   _____
> f) I enjoy learning new vocabulary items.   _____
> g) I do not like working in pairs and small groups.   _____

Try this ☞ **Survey about topics**

Look through the coursebook or syllabus for the year ahead and write the main topics on the board. Ask students to vote for their favourite topic. Create a simple bar chart or pie chart on the board to display the results. Working in pairs, students then select a topic and come up with a survey question about it. For the topic of 'school', for example, the survey question could be: *What is your favourite subject?* or *Which new subject would you most like to learn?* Students carry out their surveys, asking all of the members of the class in turn. Each pair displays their results in the form of a bar chart or pie chart.

Try this ☞ **About me**

Create a gap-fill text for students to complete about themselves. See the example below. The content and language level can be tailored to suit your students.

> **About me**
> My name is _____ and I'm from _____. I live in _____, and in my free time I usually _____. I want to learn English because _____. I think I know a lot about _____.
> I'm good at _____. I can _____. I don't know much about _____ but I'd like to know more. I can't _____ but I'd like to learn how.
> People often say that I'm _____, _____, and _____.
>
> In the future, I'd like to _____ because _____.

Feedback

A certain amount of trial and error is involved in finding the best approach for each group. Teachers can get formal or informal feedback from students on particular activities or on the lesson as a whole. This can be done either by asking them directly, or by getting students to write down a few comments, in **L1** if appropriate.

Observation

Teachers can gain useful insights into students by paying attention to how well they cope with the materials they are given, how they respond to certain activities, and how they interact with each other – especially when they think that no one is paying attention to them specifically! Informal observation of this kind essentially involves keeping our eyes and ears open during the lesson. Further examples of things to notice in students might include:

- how well they manage to focus on tasks
- how much time they need for tasks
- how willing they are to volunteer or to respond when called on
- whether they are prepared to ask for/give help.

Formal observation is also a possibility. The fresh perspective of an outside observer can help us to get a more rounded view of what is actually happening in the mixed-ability classroom. Getting a colleague to observe a lesson is not only easy to arrange, but also paves the way for the kind of mutually beneficial collaboration that occurs when colleagues share ideas and help each other openly and constructively.

Try this ☞   **Teacher predictions**

Invite a colleague to observe one or more of your classes. Choose two students that you would like to focus on. Write some notes about each student. Think about:

- attitude towards learning
- personal traits and characteristics.

Make predictions about how you think each student will respond to the activities you have planned. Write simple sentences, as in Table 1.1.

Maria	Daniel
1 I think she'll talk in L1 to her neighbours during the first activity. **Observer's comments:**	1 I think he'll copy the answers to the first activity from Luis. **Observer's comments:**
2 I think she'll be cheerful and enthusiastic about volunteering for the speaking task. **Observer's comments:**	2 I think he'll be shy and will not volunteer for the speaking task. **Observer's comments:**
3 etc.	3 etc.

TABLE 1.1   *Teacher predictions about students*

 **Getting it right**   **Observation criteria**

The observation criteria should be identified before the lesson and should be as objective as possible in order to make the job of the observer straightforward. An observation checklist should also be prepared before the lesson. It might help to make a set of predictions about certain students before the class and to discuss these with the observer. After the lesson, the predictions can be reviewed and assessed.

Why this works

Comparing predictions with outcomes

Sometimes we label or pigeonhole our students without even being aware of it. The labels we subconsciously attach to them might be things such as 'She finds it hard to concentrate' or 'He never listens'. This is a potentially harmful tendency as these labels often become self-fulfilling prophecies. Comparing predictions with outcomes helps us to find out whether or not we truly know our students as well as we like to think we do. It also helps us to get a clear idea of whether certain tasks and activities are suitable for a particular mixed-ability group.

Reflecting on data

Completed questionnaires, worksheets, and feedback forms can be referred to regularly during the course of the year when planning activities for a mixed-ability class, especially when looking for ways to involve particular individuals. When displayed on the classroom wall, survey results can act as a reminder to the teacher about topics, areas, and working methods to explore. In the case of collaboration with colleagues, follow-up observations and discussions can help to fine-tune teachers' reflections and conclusions about handling the variables within the group.

Try this

Summarizing interests

Share a summary of the data gathered from class questionnaires and worksheets and ask students to interpret it. Provide a range of helpful language for this purpose, such as: *No one likes ...* , *A few people like ...* , *Some of us like ...* , *Most people like ...* , *Everyone likes ...* . Get students to create a poster, bar chart, or pie chart to represent the preferences of the class.

2 Setting goals

Setting goals should be seen as a way of identifying strengths and areas to work on, based on the variables identified. The goals that are set should acknowledge the needs and preferences expressed by individuals, and attempt to find opportunities to engage them. At the same time, it is important to identify group goals that reflect the shared needs and preferences of the class.

There is a clear link between setting goals and achieving positive outcomes. Setting goals can focus minds, while achieving goals leads to a feeling of success. In the mixed-ability classroom, students should be given an active and participatory role to play in setting goals wherever possible, rather than always being presented with a list of goals that have been drawn up by the teacher.

We should also set goals for ourselves as teachers, making sure that we have a clear idea about the objectives we would like to meet with the group and the methods we intend to use for the purpose. This can be as simple as asking 'What am I hoping to achieve in this lesson?' and then spending a few minutes afterwards reflecting on the actual outcomes by taking brief notes.

Class goals

Goals can rarely be achieved merely by identifying desired outcomes and then hoping for the best. Instead, it is necessary to formulate the specific steps that need to be taken in order to achieve the end result we are looking for. This way, checking progress can become an established routine and an integral part of classroom procedure.

Goals can be set for single lessons or activities, in which case they should be discussed and written on the board. Alternatively, long-term objectives can be identified and displayed in the form of a poster on the classroom wall. Unless goals for mixed-ability classes are stated clearly and made public, it is hard for both teachers and students to be aware of them.

Try this ☞ **Class contract**

Goals can be as simple as guidelines and ground rules. Discuss class goals with students. This can be done in L1 if necessary. Make sure that your objectives are clear and that they have been agreed upon by everyone. Draw up a class contract such as the example opposite. The contract should focus on the steps you need to take in order to achieve the goals you and the class have set for yourselves. Sign the contract, get students to sign it as well, and display it in the classroom.

Our goals

What we want to achieve:

_____

How we intend to achieve our goals:

_____

What we are prepared to do:
- *Every lesson we will* _____
- *Every week we will* _____

We promise <u>not</u> to:

_____

Personal goals

Students should be encouraged to identify both language-learning goals and attitude goals, and to think about how they can be applied to learning both inside and outside the classroom. Examples of appropriate goals can be elicited, or teachers can supply examples by drawing on their own experience as language learners. Examples of language-learning goals might be: keeping a notebook for new words and reviewing it after every lesson, reading a newspaper article every day, or doing online grammar exercises for each completed unit in the book. Examples of attitude goals might be: arriving on time for class, not interrupting when others are speaking, or respecting the opinions of others in the group.

Try this ☞ **My personal goals**

Elicit a few examples of personal goals. Give students the template below to fill in individually.

My personal goals

By the end of the course I want to be able to ...

- _____
- _____
- _____

In order to do this, I will ...

- _____
- _____
- _____

I will spend about _____ hours this week/month/term on self-study to achieve these goals.

Signed: _____

Then put students in groups of four – their aim is to identify three common goals. Finally, discuss the common goals with the whole group. Try to come up with three or four goals for the entire class. Write them on a poster or large piece of card and put them somewhere in the classroom where they are clearly visible. Refer to them throughout the period of time that you have specified. At the end, the goals can be checked as a whole-group activity.

Try this    **Promises**

Get students to set goals for themselves at the beginning of the course. They can take the form of a promise or pledge relating to everyday behaviour, as in the example in Table 2.1. Ask students to write down their goals on a separate piece of paper. All students should be asked to consult their list of goals and check their progress at regular intervals. Students can occasionally work in pairs and review each other's goals.

Language-learning goals	Attitude goals
I promise to: • practise the pronunciation of new words using an online dictionary • read a newspaper headline every day and translate it.	I promise to: • switch my phone off in class • offer to help others whenever I can.

TABLE 2.1   *Student promises*

Try this 👉   **Goal points**

Acknowledge the importance of goal setting by allocating students points when individual and group goals have been achieved. Keep a running score of the points awarded. When students have collected an agreed number of points, they can be awarded a top grade. Alternatively, points awarded for goal achievement can be incorporated into formal assessment, for example by including a goal-achievement component in continuous assessment. (See Part 7 for more information on assessing mixed-ability groups.)

✓ *Getting it right*   **Goal setting**

The following four questions provide a basis for making sure that goals are set appropriately.

1 *Can it be done?* Each goal that learners set for themselves needs to be realistic in terms of their abilities and the time available.
2 *Is it clear?* Each goal should be expressed as specifically as possible, and preferably in terms of action points. Students should be encouraged to express their goals in a way that is easy to check.
3 *How will it be achieved?* Students need to be able to see a clear path from what they do in class to the fulfilment of the desired goal.
4 *Is it what the student wants?* A goal is only likely to be achieved if it is self-determined and reflects the desires of students themselves rather than their teachers or parents.

3

Planning differentiated activities

Differentiated activities

Providing each learner in a mixed-ability class with materials tailor-made to suit their individual level is not a practical option: it would require far too much preparation and would be extremely difficult to manage. Instead, one of the ways that we can provide multi-level input is by preparing **differentiated** language-learning activities which share the same common core. Differentiated materials do not require excessive amounts of preparation; in any case, the additional time required in the preparation phase is often repaid in terms of time saved in the classroom. The positive effects of differentiation are not always apparent to students experiencing it for the first time; they might confuse it with discrimination. In fact, differentiation enables teachers to include all students in the learning process – something that students themselves are usually quick to appreciate. It is important, however, to be sensitive to students' feelings, and to avoid discriminatory language. For example, say *the green group and the purple group* not *the strong group and the weak group*.

Differentiating the input

One possibility is to provide different learners with an activity that has been differentiated according to language level. For a reading comprehension activity, we might create two alternative versions of the text in the book: one version adapted to make it more accessible for weaker learners, and another version adapted to make it more challenging for stronger learners. Learners then tackle one of the three texts, depending on their level. See the following example:

> **Standard text**
>
> Joanne 'Jo' Rowling OBE (born 31 July 1965) is a British author who wrote the Harry Potter books. She only uses the name 'J.K. Rowling' for her books: the 'K' stands for 'Kathleen' which was the first name of her grandmother.

Think about how this text could be changed to make it more/less challenging for learners. Some ideas are overleaf.

Alternative 1 (More challenging)	Alternative 2 (Less challenging)
1 Use gaps	5 Use simpler synonyms
2 Use more difficult synonyms	6 Use images
3 Use anagrams	7 Use L1
4 Provide more text to read	8 Add explanations to help understanding

The skeleton texts below include examples of all the options listed above for illustrative purposes. When adapting a text to use in the classroom, it is advisable to choose one option for each text in the interests of simplicity.

Alternative 1

Joanne 'Jo' Rowling OBE (born 31 July 1965) is a British author who wrote the Harry Potter books. She [1]o_____ uses the [2]*pseudonym* 'J.K. Rowling' for her books: the 'K' stands for 'Kathleen' which was the first name of her [3]*monthgrader*.

[4](She received a degree in French and Classics at the University of Exeter. She worked at Amnesty International in London. The original idea for Harry Potter came to her on a train in 1990.)

Alternative 2

[6] Joanne 'Jo' Rowling OBE (born 31 July 1965) is a British [5]writer who wrote the Harry Potter books. She only uses [7]*használja* the name 'J.K. Rowling' for her books: the 'K' stands for [8](=) 'Kathleen' which was the first name of her grandmother.

Differentiating the process

Another way of differentiating is to give students alternative ways of working with the same input, for example a set of questions. Students can then be given three separate ways of finding the answers to the questions: by reading a text, by completing a spoken information gap activity, or by doing individual research.

Here we are not differentiating the level of the input language. Instead, we are providing different options regarding how it is used – enabling students to work in their own way, at their own level, and at their own pace. See the example opposite.

All of the students in the group receive the same questions about the tallest building in the world:

> **The tallest building in the world**
> 1 Which city is it in?
> 2 What is it called?
> 3 How many metres high is it?
> 4 How many floors has it got?

The teacher then differentiates by providing three varieties of input material.

> **Group A: Reading comprehension**
>
> **Read the text and find the answers.**
>
> Dubai, in the United Arab Emirates, is different from other cities. It is a city of glass skyscrapers in the desert. One of these is the incredible Burj Khalifa skyscraper. It is 828 metres high and has got more than 160 floors. You can see it from 100 kilometres away!
>
> *English Plus Student's Book 1*, Oxford University Press
>
> **Group B: Information gap**
>
> **Read the text. It contains two of the answers. Then ask someone from Group C to read their text to you. Listen and write the missing information.**
>
> _____, in the United Arab Emirates, is different from other cities. It is a city of glass skyscrapers in the desert. One of these is the incredible Burj Khalifa skyscraper. It is _____ metres high and has got more than 160 floors. You can see it from 100 kilometres away!
>
> **Group C: Information gap**
>
> **Read the text. It contains two of the answers. Then ask someone from Group B to read their text to you. Listen and write in the missing information.**
>
> Dubai, in the United Arab Emirates, is different from other cities. It is a city of glass skyscrapers in the desert. One of these is the incredible _____ skyscraper. It is 828 metres high and has got more than _____ floors. You can see it from 100 kilometres away!
>
> **Group D: Individual research**
>
> **Find the answers to the questions by using the internet.**

Differentiating the output

Differentiating the output allows students to engage with topics in their own way by responding to **open questions** and prompts, rather than **closed questions**. In such cases, students do not all produce the same outcome. If we let students activate their own preferences and use the language they already know, then more personalized outcomes are possible. The teacher can then evaluate this work on its individual merits.

In order for this to work, we need to provide a common topic, but be flexible in the way we use it as the starting point for **open-ended tasks**. One way that this can be done is to give students a set amount of time in which to generate as much relevant language as they can. Another way is to provide a menu of tasks at different levels from which students are free to choose the option that most appeals to them.

Try this    **At the market**

Give students the following task for homework.

> **Go to the fruit and vegetables section of a market/supermarket near your home. Choose <u>one</u> of these tasks:**
>
> 1 Write down the names of as many of the fruits and vegetables as you can in English. Use your phone to take photos of them and finish the task at home.
> 2 Which fruit/vegetable is ...
>
> | | |
> |---|---|
> | a the most expensive? | e the heaviest? |
> | b the cheapest? | f the longest? |
> | c the most delicious? | g the ugliest? |
> | d the most beautiful? | h not from your country? |
>
> 3 Interview the person selling the fruits and vegetables – or the people buying them. Use your phone to record the interview. Translate the questions and answers into English.

✓ *Getting it right*   **Assigning differentiated tasks to students**

When using differentiated activities in the classroom, resist the temptation to always assign certain tasks to particular learners. Very often it is not the differentiation itself that concerns students, but the fact that they do not have a say in how the allocation is made.

Deciding when to differentiate

The question of <u>when</u> to differentiate needs to be considered within the context of the lesson as a whole. Looking through the lesson plan and anticipating how students will respond to each activity can provide the basis for decisions regarding when to differentiate. When you do so, ask yourself the following questions:

1 Are students provided with choices and options at any time in this lesson?
2 Are there any opportunities for getting students to help each other in this lesson?
3 Are there any activities that might be problematic?
4 Are there any ways of making these activities more open-ended?

It is also important to consider the stage of the lesson and the **transitions** between activities. Differentiated activities can be used to change the **flow** of a lesson, for example to enable freer practice or creative language use following a closed activity.

✓ *Getting it right*   **When <u>not</u> to differentiate**

It is important to remember that beginning and ending the class together is very important from the point of view of classroom dynamics. It sends a strong signal to the group of inclusiveness and togetherness. For this reason, it makes sense <u>not</u> to use differentiated activities at the very start of the lesson or right at the end.

Part 2   Managing the classroom

4   Grouping students

Benefits of grouping

Frontal teaching does little to address the differences of level in mixed-ability groups. Trying to get learners to learn in **lockstep** mode does not account for differences in rates of learning or allow individuals to work according to their particular needs and preferences.

Whole-class activities can be fun and engaging for learners, but if this is the only mode of instruction then frustration can mount. Stronger learners can become restless and weaker learners often get left behind. In addition, the feeling of being an anonymous member of the class can lead to passive behaviour.

When learners in mixed-ability groups are given activities to tackle in small groups and pairs, however, there are more opportunities for personalized learning. Not only can learners get more help and assistance, but working in smaller groups provides more chances for language activation.

In whole-class activities, being called on to give a response can make weaker learners feel as if they are being singled out. In the long-term, there are constructive ways to bring about a shift in learners' attitudes towards questions asked in frontal mode (see Chapter 6), but anxiety among weaker learners is difficult to overcome. Using pair-work and group-work activities on a regular basis remains the surest way of building learner confidence and achieving optimal levels of participation.

Pair work and group work also offer greater variety within activities, allowing individual students to work together with a number of different classmates in the same lesson and, over the course of a term, with everyone in the class.

Options for grouping

Grouping learners of the same level together

One way of grouping learners is to put those of similar language level together, enabling the teacher to prepare input materials that have been differentiated to suit their needs. In this way, learners can be provided with extra support and can also benefit from further explanations, if necessary. A further advantage of this way of grouping is that learners who are intimidated by the superior knowledge of the stronger members of the class are provided with a secure space in which they can work with fewer inhibitions.

Stronger learners can be provided with additional challenges that allow them to work autonomously when they are grouped together. This also frees the teacher to focus more on providing weaker learners with help and assistance.

Grouping learners of different levels together

Another way of grouping is to put learners of different language levels together, ensuring that each small group contains both stronger and weaker learners. This encourages learners to help each other and learn from each other, while also enabling other important skills and attitudes, such as social skills and tolerance, to be developed.

Because the emphasis is much more on students helping each other, the teacher's role is more of a facilitator than an instructor. Although mixed groups offer rich opportunities for collaboration and cooperation between students, it is important to monitor the interaction and provide reassurance to both stronger and weaker learners.

A further advantage of mixed groups is that they provide a more lifelike context for communication, in which language skills and interpersonal skills need to be combined.

Other options

Grouping does not have to be determined by language level. In project work, for example, choice of topic can be the criterion for grouping. If the given topic is 'free-time activities', and five students in the class express an interest in football, it makes sense to put them together to work on a project about their favourite sport. Their shared interest in the topic means they are more likely to be motivated, and the grouping feels natural and uncontrived even if there are differences in language level between the members of the group.

Occasionally, you might wish to group students randomly. Random groupings provide variety and ensure that students do not always work with the same people in pair-work and group-work activities.

Techniques for grouping

It is common to form groups by asking students to work with the people sitting next to them or near them. Although convenient, it tends to result in students always working with the same people. If students always work with the same people, motivation levels tend to drop and **off-task behaviour** tends to increase. It is worth experimenting with other techniques, especially if we would like to engineer groupings according to language criteria.

The grouping procedure can be an engaging activity in its own right, providing plenty of opportunities for communication. Grouping techniques are not only effective classroom tools, they are also a great way to get students' attention and raise interest in the activity that is to follow.

Naturally, some groupings will be more successful than others. With time, and as students get to know each other better, you will be able to find a system that works best for you and for them. Working with others certainly means that students will need to learn to compromise. Although this might be difficult for them on occasions, it is precisely the kind of life skill that will benefit them outside the classroom. Students who are initially reluctant to collaborate should be reminded of the benefits of this skill in real life, and provided with praise and encouragement for their efforts.

Try this ☞ **Grab the string**

This is a fun way to get students into pairs. Before class, get a roll of string and cut it into pieces about 30 cm long. You will need one piece of string for every two students in the group. Put all the string together and hold the bunch in the middle. Invite students to grab the end of one of the pieces of string. When everyone has taken hold, let go of the bunch. Students find whoever is holding the other end of their piece of string and work with that person.

Try this ☞ **Coloured sticky notes**

Use different-coloured sticky notes or small coloured cards to group students simply and effectively. Place a sticky note on each student's desk before the lesson to save time. Random and 'engineered' groupings are both possible using this method.

Try this ☞ **Sorting activity**

Set all students the same activity (e.g. a topic quiz, a timed vocabulary-matching task, a multiple-choice grammar exercise, etc.) and correct it. On the basis of the results, decide how students are going to be grouped for the next activity that you have planned. The sorting activity can be used to gain a quick indication of how well the students have understood a certain language point, or to see how much background information they have about a topic. In each case, this information can help the teacher decide about subsequent groupings more effectively.

Try this ☞ **Onion groups**

Students work on a task or activity in groups of three or four. When the teacher gives the signal, one member of the group 'peels off' and goes to join another group, where information is exchanged. The 'peelers' continue around the room at regular intervals, finally returning to their original group after visiting all of the other groups in the room.

Onion grouping can work well in situations where each group has been given slightly different information to work with. Only by pooling resources can each group get the 'full picture' and complete the task.

Try this ☞ **Autograph book**

Get students to create an 'autograph book' for keeping track of who they work with in group situations. They do not need to have a separate book for this – it can easily be done on the back page of their exercise book. Their job is to collect the signature of each partner in their book at the conclusion of the activity. Think of a small prize or reward for the student who eventually manages to work with everyone else in the class. This technique is designed to ensure that students do not always work with the same partner in situations where there is a lot of group work and pair work.

5 Learner roles

Day-to-day involvement

Managing the classroom is the responsibility of the teacher – but that does not mean that students should be completely excluded from the process. In fact, there are many ways that we can involve students meaningfully in the day-to-day running of the classroom by finding appropriate roles for them to perform.

In the mixed-ability classroom, tasks that are not directly connected to language learning provide weaker or less motivated students with the opportunity to make an important contribution to the lesson. Providing less confident students with chances to help and provide assistance during the lesson also creates opportunities for them to be praised for their contributions and recognized for their efforts.

Try this ☞ **Timekeeper**

It can be hard to administer activities while keeping an eye on the clock. When you are doing an activity that has to be finished in a specified amount of time, get one of the students to be the timekeeper. Their responsibility is to monitor the time spent on the activity, and to let the teacher know when the allotted time is up.

Decision-making

Besides getting students to help with routine tasks and duties, we can also explore ways of delegating some of the decision-making to our students. Everyone benefits from such an approach. The teacher saves time and effort; the students feel valued and involved.

Try this ☞ **Dice master**

Involve students in the classroom decision-making process by occasionally inviting one of them to be the 'dice master'. Whenever there is a minor decision to take (e.g. listening to a song more than once), the nominated student can roll the dice. The dice master announces the rules (e.g. *If it's 1, 2, or 3, we listen again. If it's 4, 5, or 6, we don't*) and then rolls the dice to decide the outcome.

Why this works ⫸

> **Student inclusion in decision-making**
> Students really enjoy being included in these decision-making processes, and they also benefit from the boost to their self-esteem which comes from being nominated by the teacher. With the dice-master activity, the dice determine the outcome of the decision-making process – not the student or the teacher!

Roles that boost confidence

The transition from being a passive member of the group to that of being an active learner requires a change in learners' attitudes about themselves and their roles within the classroom. It is not an easy process, and few learners are able to do it unassisted. Members of the group can develop confidence and self-belief through carrying out useful roles. As their confidence develops, their capacity to see themselves as active learners is also enhanced. Teachers also benefit from seeing them in a new light.

Try this ☞   **Who's going to clean the board?**

Get a student to clean the board instead of doing it yourself, especially with groups of younger learners. Nominate someone who you would like to single out for special praise. For example, it might be an easily distracted student who concentrated much better than usual. Focus on a different attribute or criterion each time you nominate a student to clean the board, noticing examples of individual improvement or improved effort in each case. If you use an interactive whiteboard, apply the same principle when inviting students to come out to drag-and-drop, write, or draw on it.

Why this works ⫸

> **Students cleaning the board**
>
> Cleaning the board can be problematic from a classroom-management perspective: the teacher's back is turned, the students are waiting, nothing much is happening. This is often the point in a lesson when students become restless or distracted. Being chosen to clean the board helps students feel that their efforts and performance are being appreciated, and that the teacher is paying attention to what they are doing as individuals. It also frees the teacher to focus on setting up the next activity.

Making suggestions and providing expertise

As learners' confidence grows, they can begin to take on roles which go beyond that of helping the teacher and focus instead on taking responsibility for their own learning. One way that we can do this is by asking them to play a more active role in determining how activities are organized and by asking them to think constructively about how the lesson could be managed to the greater benefit of themselves and other learners. After a speaking activity, for example, learners could be asked: *Did this activity help your speaking? How?* As a follow-up, they could be asked: *Can you suggest any changes or improvements?* These questions can be discussed in L1 if it seems more natural.

Initially, learners expect the teacher to be the 'expert' and are usually reluctant to offer an opinion. Over time, however, they will gradually become more willing to share their views, especially if they see that their suggestions are welcomed by the teacher – and acted on. As an example, imagine that we are interested in hearing students' views on how homework is checked in class. In order to provide a basis for comparison, we might decide to try out a new, more active way of checking homework, for instance by getting students to check each other's work. Afterwards, we could ask: *Which way of checking the homework do you prefer? Why? Can you think of another way that you think would work better?*

Try this ☞ **Fact checker**

Get a less confident student to prepare a short talk about themselves, based on a set of questions provided in advance. The other students listen and then write down six sentences about the speaker. When they have finished, the speaker goes round to check that what has been written is factually correct. Students then read out one sentence each about the speaker, without repeating anything that has already been said.

Try this ☞ **Student observers**

In order to get feedback on how well a classroom management technique is working in class, invite two members of the group to be observers for a lesson. Beforehand, explain what you would like them to focus on – the use of the 'traffic light cups' for instance (see Chapter 6). After the lesson, sit down with the two students to hear their observations, including any suggestions they might have for improving how the cups are used in class.

6

Teacher roles

Facilitating involvement

The key role of the teacher in mixed-ability groups is that of facilitating learning by enabling individuals of all levels and abilities to feel sufficiently challenged in the lesson. It is the responsibility of the teacher to reach out to all learners, making sure that they not only understand what is being asked of them, but also that they are involved and motivated to take part. The teacher also needs to oversee the balance of individual involvement, making sure that everyone is provided with equal opportunities for participation.

Making sure students can follow

Explanations by the teacher to the whole group need to be clearly understandable, particularly when it comes to giving instructions for activities. Weaker or less confident learners might require additional input, while stronger learners need to be kept engaged.

Try this ☞ **Lesson checklist**
On the board, write a list of the activities you have planned for the lesson.
At the start of the class, get all students to write it down in their exercise books.
Describe what is going to happen and what students are going to be doing.
As you complete each activity, cross it off on the board – and get students to do the same in their books.

Creating options and openings for involvement

Prompts from the teacher should aim to include learners rather than exclude them. Open-ended questions are inclusive as they enable a variety of valid responses. Closed questions, on the other hand, are more likely to exclude learners from offering a response. For this reason, open-ended prompts and tasks are much better at promoting involvement than closed questions. Offering students a selection of tasks to choose from is another effective way of promoting involvement and is more likely to generate a willing response.

Try this ☞ **Open-ended weekend review**

At the start of the week, instead of asking *Did you have a good weekend?*, write several open-ended prompts on the board. For example:

● Describe someone or something that made you smile this weekend.

● Which part of the weekend was the most boring? Why?

Allow learners to choose which prompt they would like to respond to and provide them with time to prepare their answer. Invite them to work with a partner and share their responses. Then ask for volunteers to read out their answers.

Accommodating learners of different levels

One of the most difficult aspects of the teacher's role in the mixed-ability classroom is finding a way to make input both accessible and relevant to learners of different language levels. Pitching the lesson halfway between the levels of the strongest and weakest learners in the group will <u>not</u> guarantee that everyone is optimally engaged: for some, the input will be too challenging; for others, it will be too easy. On the other hand, such an approach makes intuitive sense: if input is pitched in the middle of the range, it is immediately accessible to a higher proportion of students, while weaker and stronger learners can be provided with the additional support and extra challenges that they require.

Stronger learners

The needs and abilities of stronger learners should not be allowed to set the agenda for the whole group. Instead, stronger learners can be provided with extension activities and further challenges in the form of optional tasks for fast finishers. However, it is important that they receive meaningful feedback on the outcomes of their work, either orally or in writing.

Weaker learners

Providing differentiated activities is an effective way to give weaker learners additional support and guidance, but only if they are receptive to the concept that differentiation is not intended to be discriminatory. It is important for students to see that our aim is to provide them access to language that is meaningful for <u>them</u>. Weaker learners might feel that doing differentiated activities means that they are being left out. In fact, we need to communicate that our aim is to find ways to include them in the lesson, not exclude them.

Promoting learning in frontal teaching

Pair work and group work can activate students' learning effectively, but we also need to consider the broader context of classroom interaction. A considerable proportion of class time is still going to be spent in frontal mode: introducing topics, explaining language points, checking understanding, setting up activities, reviewing outcomes, etc. It is essential that all learners are engaged during frontal modes of instruction, but this is not always the case.

Limitations of 'hands up'

Traditional frontal teaching consists of the teacher talking and asking questions. Students listen and volunteer to answer questions by raising their hands. Recent research suggests that the traditional 'hands up' system typically activates only 25% of a mixed-ability group: the stronger students regularly put their hands up; the majority of students, however, assume a passive role.

How can the remaining 75% of the class be activated? One way is by experimenting with a 'no hands up' policy and using an alternative technique, such as randomizing the procedure for deciding who answers questions in class.

Try this ☞   **Lollipop sticks**

Write the name of each student on a lollipop stick and keep them in a jar on your desk. Whenever you ask a question, instead of calling students based on whether or not they have their hands up, choose a lollipop stick at random from the jar and call on that student.

Why this works ⫸

> **Lollipop sticks**
>
> The lollipop stick technique guarantees that all students have an equal opportunity to answer questions and helps weaker learners to become involved in the lesson. It also keeps students on their toes – they never know when they might be asked a question! A further benefit is that it encourages stronger learners to wait their turn and pay more attention to the contributions of others in the group. They might also have the unusual (and arguably healthy) experience of being asked a question to which they do not know the answer, helping them to become more aware of their own specific learning needs.

It is also important to provide students with non-verbal ways to show how well they are coping with activities. We can do this by providing them with the means to signal how well they understand an explanation, and to indicate whether or not they are having difficulties or require extra help. The 'traffic lights' activity is a good way of achieving this.

Try this ☞   **Traffic lights**

Give each student a set of three plastic cups: one green, one orange, and one red. The cups are stacked and placed on each student's desk. When asked by the teacher, students restack their cups to indicate their status: a green cup on top means there are no problems or questions, an orange cup on top means that not everything is clear, a red cup on top signals that the learner needs help.

Why this works ⫸

> **Traffic lights**
>
> This is a simple way of getting a group status update. It can also make giving remedial instruction more efficient: learners displaying a red cup can be put together before receiving extra explanation from the teacher. It also enables **team learning**, as those who are having difficulties can seek the help of a learner with a green cup on the top of their stack.

*Getting it right*

Explaining changes

Students and teachers are so used to the 'hands up' system that this technique can take some getting used to for both students and teachers. Explain to students why the system is being introduced. It is important to stress that getting an answer wrong is fine, and to enforce a 'zero tolerance' policy regarding students making fun of incorrect answers given by others in the group. Stronger learners are likely to be frustrated by not being able to answer as many questions as before. For this reason, use of the mini-whiteboards technique (see Chapter 15) is recommended in classrooms where the 'no hands up' rule is being used, so that everyone has a chance to show the teacher their answers.

Communicating the approach to others

Colleagues, parents, and educational managers might not fully understand or agree with the approach to classroom management described in this chapter. The most effective way to gain their support is to provide opportunities for them to experience the methods first-hand.

Try this ☞ **Demo lesson for parents**

Invite parents to attend a special demonstration lesson in which you showcase some of the techniques that you would like them to support. Parents sit with their children and take part in the lesson actively. The lesson itself does not have to be in English!

Appreciating the whole person

In Chapter 24 we discuss a **whole-person approach** to teaching mixed-ability groups. If learners of different abilities are going to thrive, it is vital that teachers assume the role of enablers in the day-to-day business of running the classroom. We can do this by encouraging students to listen to each other, by helping them to understand and connect with each other, and by allowing them to share their own expertise. Teachers, too, should reveal that they are more than just language instructors.

Try this ☞ **Teacher anecdotes**

When introducing a new topic, share any interesting personal stories you have in connection with it. Students particularly appreciate stories that are funny or show the teacher in a new light. For example, before a lesson on the subject of cooking, describe a disastrous experience you once had in the kitchen!

7 Creating a positive learning environment

Affirmation and positive reinforcement

Creating a positive learning environment is especially important in a mixed-ability setting, where there are so many different needs, strengths, and personalities. The way we manage our lessons has a huge impact on the kind of learning environment that emerges. A positive learning environment can be best achieved if all of the students receive affirmation of their value and positive reinforcement in response to their efforts, not only from the teacher but also from one another.

Building a sense of team learning can have a positive effect on how students feel about themselves individually, and also as members of the group. Providing a meaningful reward for collective effort is one way of achieving this, especially if it has to be negotiated.

Try this ☞ **'Killing' vocab items**

Reward students by getting the class to look at a list of words which they have to learn for a vocabulary test and giving them the option of 'killing' any three items. In groups, ask them to decide which three words they consider to be the most difficult to learn, and why. Go round each group in turn. Write their selections on the board and listen to what they have to say. When the class has reached a final decision, make sure that these words do <u>not</u> appear in the next vocabulary test.

Why this works ▥▶

> **'Killing' vocab items**
>
> The reward on offer suits both students and the teacher. Students are happy that the three most difficult words are not on the test. The teacher also benefits because – paradoxically – students will almost certainly have learnt those three words as a result of the classroom discussion!

As we have indicated before, the beginning and end of the lesson are key moments in which to be aware of the learning environment in the mixed-ability classroom and to think about how we can try to shape it. Beginning the lesson by offering students an incentive establishes a positive frame of mind, while the promise of something to look forward to later in the lesson improves focus and sustains group motivation. For teenagers, incentives can be brainteasers or general knowledge questions that the group needs to solve together. Younger learners can be offered a mystery to solve, such as recognizing an animal from an audio recording, or identifying an object inside a box by touch. Saving the chosen treat for the end of the lesson gives you the chance to decide whether or not it has been deserved, and it also gives students a chance to finish the lesson on a high.

There is also potential for classroom routines that enable individual students to be singled out by the rest of the group for rewards. When students decide together which member of the group most deserves recognition, the value of such a reward is amplified considerably. Furthermore, the act of awarding a small privilege to a classmate strengthens the culture of affirmation and improves the group dynamic.

Try this ☞ **Who can leave first?**

Give one student the chance to be the first to leave the classroom at the end of the lesson. Ask the whole class to decide which one of them most deserves this privilege based on specific criteria. You might ask: *Who has been the most helpful today?* or *Which one of you asked the best question today?* Get students to vote, and allow the one who gets the most votes to gather their things and leave first, with the others having to wait a little longer.

✓ *Getting it right*

Who can leave first?

This technique does not actually involve letting certain students leave much earlier, or keeping others back. It simply focuses on the order in which they can leave the room. A few seconds' head start on the others is often more than enough to make most students happy.

An effective approach to discipline

A perennial challenge of teaching in mixed-ability groups is handling behaviour problems. Traditional approaches to discipline tend to be based on establishing deterrents and handing out punishment for undesirable behaviour, which fail to tackle the root of the problem and do very little to improve the learning environment. A more effective approach to discipline is called for, one that focuses instead on positive reinforcement of desirable behaviour. Over time, it is usually possible to achieve gradual improvements in student behaviour by providing students with opportunities to self-correct and by using the positive power of peer pressure.

Offering chances to self-correct

Not all disruptive behaviour is intentional. The chattering, fidgeting, and giggling of distracted or restless students is an annoyance when it interferes with our teaching, but it is important to recognize that all students have occasional lapses of focus. On these occasions, students need to see that we have noticed their behaviour and are keen for it to stop. They should, however, be given a chance to self-correct their behaviour before we take measures to address the problem ourselves.

Try this ☞ **Are you thirsty?**

If a student's restlessness is proving to be disruptive, suggest that they leave the classroom briefly to have a drink of water. Speak firmly, but without scolding or showing frustration. When the student returns, do not say anything. Continue teaching. The next time the student begins behaving in a restless or distracted way, simply ask: *Are you thirsty?* Usually, they get the message.

 *Getting it right*

Dealing with distracted students

It is important to note that this technique will not fix the behaviour of students whose disruptive behaviour is intentional; it will, however, act as an effective 'heads up' to students who have momentarily become distracted – a common phenomenon in every mixed-ability classroom.

Dealing with 'problem students'

There are certain students whose behaviour in class is a regular cause of disruption. We might find that we consistently have to interrupt our teaching to deal directly with discipline issues connected to the same student, who often appears unwilling or unable to accept the opportunities we offer to self-correct. This is both detrimental to the learning environment and extremely frustrating for all concerned.

Although it can be hard, a positive approach to dealing with such situations is essential if we want to maintain a healthy learning environment. In Chapter 23 we discuss the link between thoughts, feelings, and behaviour, and it is by focusing on the whole student rather than just their behaviour that we can achieve the best outcomes.

Try this ☞ **Two-by-ten**

The psychologist Raymond Wlodkowski suggests a strategy of engaging the same student in two minutes of conversation after class, for ten lessons in a row. The conversation can be in L1 and should not be defensive or confrontational. Stick to general topics not directly connected to the student's behaviour.

Why this works ▶ **Two-by-ten**

Students whose behaviour is disruptive or problematic often have a sense of 'not being heard' or that the teacher does not care about them. The two-by-ten strategy allows both the teacher and student to see each other in a new light. Tension that might have been building up between the two can begin to be defused. There is no guarantee that this technique will work for every student, but it can be a highly effective way of developing cooperation between the teacher and a problem student. A positive change in that student's behaviour often results by the end of the tenth chat. And if the student in question is seen as something of a role model by others in the group, the change in their behaviour can spread to others in the group as well.

Part 3   Making the most of L1

8   Making ourselves understood

Teacher language

There are still differing views and practices regarding the use of L1 in the English language classroom and, at the risk of overgeneralizing, they can be categorized in three ways:

1 teachers who completely avoid using or may be unable to use the native language (L1)
2 teachers who use it sparingly
3 teachers who use it regularly and liberally.

Before reading on, stop for a moment and reflect on which category you think you might fall into and why. Then consider the following questions for each category.

- Do you want to give students the most exposure to English? Are you influenced in any way by your pre-service teacher-training course or strong beliefs set by others? How?
- Do you have any criteria for using L1? What are they?
- What do you consider to be beneficial about this approach?

It might be time to reconsider our views about using L1 in the classroom. Although it is true that exclusive use of the target language in the classroom provides maximum exposure to English, this approach also has several drawbacks. As soon as lower-level learners fail to grasp instructions or comments from the teacher, they feel excluded from large parts of the lesson, leading to greater insecurity, a sense of isolation, and a drop in self-confidence. This can widen the gap between group members in terms of linguistic competence and put further strain on the social dynamics of the group itself. In settings where learners and the teacher share the same native language, L1 can be a hugely effective tool for promoting understanding, involvement, and confidence.

Successful communication depends on clarity of understanding and natural interaction. In order to ensure that all learners understand the language of the classroom, L1 can be used selectively to support what is said in English by the teacher. In a mixed-ability classroom, using L1 for more complex instructions and occasional personal comments keeps the lesson running smoothly in a natural way and can help all students to stay engaged throughout the lesson.

Try this 👉 **Helping with instructions**

Give instructions in English, then ask for a volunteer to explain what it is going to happen in L1.

Using L1 or not

A number of factors need to be considered when deciding whether or not to use L1.

- **Time:** Would it be more efficient to use L1 at this stage of the lesson?
- **Energy:** Do students need a few 'English-free moments' to recharge their batteries?
- **Mood:** Does there appear to be a problem? Would reverting to L1 help to deal with this situation efficiently?
- **Individual needs:** Does this student need personal support or encouragement from the teacher?
- **Motives for students using L1:** Is this student unwilling or unable to continue in English?

Try this 👉 **Sandwiching**

If there is a key word or phrase that you want all students to understand, say it three times: first in English, then in L1, and finally in English again. Make a conscious effort to use this technique with the same word or phrase a few times until students acquire it. Eventually, you can try giving instructions in English only.

Try this 👉 **L1-to-English feedback**

Get feedback in L1 first so that students respond to the text or the activity as freely as possible. Then reformulate each idea into English together. This could serve as a summary of their own thoughts in English.

Learner language

Needless to say, teachers would like learners to speak in English as much as possible. L1 is part of our identity, however, and by forbidding learners from using it, we are denying them access to themselves. In the mixed-ability classroom, a 'zero tolerance' attitude towards the use of L1 leads to weaker learners feeling voiceless, and therefore discouraged and helpless. It is essential to equip them with the necessary tools to express their thoughts and ideas to the teacher as well as to each other.

It is natural for students to show their engagement with the content of the lesson by making remarks in L1 and offering personal anecdotes. It is better to allow them to do this in L1 than preventing them from saying anything. Comments made in L1 should be responded to in English, if possible. In this way students feel that their ideas are valued.

Another practical way to help learners make the gradual switch from expressing their thoughts in L1 to expressing them in English is to provide them with easy access to the language they lack.

Try this ☞ **Personal phrasebook**

This is an ongoing collection of the occasional comments students make in L1 translated into English. Listen to what students say and write some of their recurring phrases in English on a flipchart at the side of the room. At the end of the lesson, take a few minutes to drill each phrase and revisit its meaning. Do this on a regular basis, revising the phrases cumulatively. Get learners to create their own personal phrasebook by copying each phrase into a section of their notebook reserved for the purpose. As an alternative, fast finishers could be given the task of collecting and translating the phrases.

Try this ☞ **Gap fill**

Create and give students a quick gap-fill activity where they have to use phrases from their personal phrasebook to substitute the missing words. You could also ask fast finishers to create such gap-fill sentences for each other.

Try this ☞ **Putting phrases to use**

During the last few minutes of your lesson, set a random topic for students to talk about. Ask them to look at their personal phrasebook and use at least three of the phrases as naturally as possible during the discussion.

✓ *Getting it right* **Encouraging use of English**

Be aware that some students may take advantage of situations when they are allowed to use L1 and avoid making the extra effort to use English even when this is not beyond their capacity. In these cases, indicate in advance that you would like them to use English as much as possible. Also, you could ask them to actively refer to their own personal phrasebook while speaking.

Why this works ⫸ **Personal phrasebook**

With the approach of using a personal phrasebook, learners see that the teacher is really listening to what they have to say. As a result, they become more motivated to respond when they are called on to speak. Also, it is more likely that they will be able to remember the English equivalents of their own phrases, given that they already have 'ownership' of the ideas and opinions which lay behind them.

9

From L1 to English

L1 as a learning tool

In some cases, permitting the use of the native language not only saves time and effort, it also eliminates the anxiety associated with uncertainty. With L1, we can speed up the process of clarification, enrich the value of practice, and enable learners to have instant access to the meaning and use of the new language with which they are working.

The use of L1 as a learning tool can also serve as a way to energize and involve learners of different abilities at the same time. Translation activities, when used carefully, can boost learners' understanding, and help them both to notice language in focus and also to reproduce it.

Try this 👉 **Mediating**

We often use role plays to give learners spoken fluency practice. One way to engage less able learners effectively is by devising activities based on common real-life situations, in which L1 utterances have to be translated into English. In activities of this kind, students are able to use L1 but are also given opportunities to notice the language they would like to use in English. In order to set them up:

1 Elicit real-life situations where a third person helps to overcome a communication barrier between two people, such as a bilingual shopper who intervenes between an English-speaking tourist and a shop assistant who doesn't speak English. Write the ideas on the board.

2 Put learners in groups of three and let them choose one of the three roles: the English speaker, the L1 speaker, and the mediator (who will be translating the main message of what is being said between L1 and English).

3 Ask the groups to choose one problem situation from the board and role play it. Encourage the mediator to use body language and mime, as appropriate, to illustrate the main message of each sentence. Set a time limit for the task.

4 Once the groups have finished, ask them to choose a different problem situation to act out or repeat the same situation, but this time with learners changing roles.

✔ *Getting it right*

Allocating roles carefully

You could choose to allocate the roles for the first round of role plays yourself, asking weaker learners to be the L1 speakers. This gives them the opportunity to notice how their sentences are formulated in English, while still feeling safe. If the classroom is big enough, ask learners to stand up in three rows with the mediators in the middle, so that the English speaker and the L1 speaker are as far away from each other as possible. As soon as they can't hear each other, the mediator has a real reason to help them communicate.

Try this ☞ **What does it look like in your language?**

Give students familiar sentences in English to work with, for example sentences they have already encountered in class. The words of each sentence should be on separate pieces of paper. Ask students to discuss what each sentence would look like in their own language. They can use the cards to show differences in word order, words that are not used, and extra words that are added in either of the languages.

Try this ☞ **Double translations**

Put students into mixed pairs to examine a short coursebook text or any text you have already worked with. Ask them to translate it into L1. Allow the use of both monolingual and bilingual dictionaries at this stage. Collect the scripts without further comment. Return the L1 texts several lessons later, by which time students will have forgotten what they wrote. Ask them to translate the texts back into English. At this stage they will need to help each other to remember the chunks of English together by comparing their notes. When comparing the original with their own version, students will be able to notice and discuss differences and similarities in language use.

Dictionary skills

As demonstrated above, dictionaries can provide learners in a mixed-ability classroom with an extra resource during language work. A key benefit of using dictionaries is that they allow learners to become more autonomous by enabling them to find appropriate words or usage, to confirm that they are right, to find more suitable synonyms, etc.

It is vital that we equip learners with efficient ways of using dictionaries in order to assist their learning during the lessons as well as outside the classroom. We need to raise their awareness of how to use online and printed monolingual and bilingual dictionaries.

Try this ☞ **Lost in translation**

Working in mixed groups, students are given sentences in L1 that have been poorly translated into English by students from a different class. Include a variety of **errors** that are related to multiple meaning, connotation, collocation, spelling, usage, etc. List different types of dictionaries on the board such as an online bilingual dictionary and an online monolingual dictionary (e.g. Oxford Advanced Learner's Dictionary), and give out printed dictionaries of the same type, including thesaurus dictionaries. Ask students to check and correct each sentence using the dictionaries. During feedback, elicit efficient strategies for using dictionaries to avoid such mistranslations. For example, where to look for good example sentences with the word in question, how to check the contexts in which the word is used, etc.

✓ *Getting it right*

Focusing on the strategy

Dictionary usage strategies for L1-to-English translation activities should focus on checking and cross-checking meaning. Once a potential English word has been found using a bilingual dictionary, its meaning should be cross-checked by looking up the same word in a monolingual dictionary. The words chosen for this awareness-raising activity should be easy for all students in the group, so that the focus is on working out successful strategies rather than the meaning of the words in question.

A gentle nudge

While the use of L1 is a helpful resource for both weaker and stronger students during language work, it is also key that we find ways to give them a gentle nudge towards using more English. These opportunities will not only give them more language practice, but will also enable students of all abilities to feel comfortable about taking on new and gradually more demanding challenges.

One practical way of doing this is by introducing visual stimuli.

Try this ☞ **Reversible flag**

Make a double-sided sign showing the UK or the US flag on one side and the flag of the country where you teach on the reverse. Use the flag to indicate moments when students may – but do not have to – use L1. This can be a very reassuring lifeline, particularly for students who are struggling at that particular time. Turning the flag to its 'English' side can be an effective stimulus to encourage more use of the target language.

Techniques that allow for further control of the amount of L1 used in the classroom, as in the activity below, can be an effective way of ensuring personalized differentiation as well as providing a safety net for less able students.

Try this ☞ **L1 cards**

Cut up a set of seven to ten small cards for every learner and hand them out at the beginning of the lesson. Each card can be used by the student when they want to say something in L1. Whenever they use their native language, they have to hand in one of their L1 cards. At the end of the lesson, give the cards you have collected back to students so that they can use them in subsequent lessons. After a few weeks, you may want to ask stronger students if they think they are ready to manage with one less card, gradually encouraging them to use fewer and fewer cards, i.e. to rely more on English. Alternatively, you could ask learners how many L1 cards they would like for a particular week.

Part 4   Working with language

10 New language

Helping learners understand new language

Language only makes sense if it is contextualized meaningfully, otherwise it can be confusing for learners. They also need to gain control of the new language for themselves and to feel secure when using it. In order to achieve this in a mixed-ability group, learners need to be assisted by additional 'anchors' that help them to <u>see</u> the context and grasp the meaning of new language through visual representations.

You can introduce context and represent new language through images and simple objects, such as Lego pieces or buttons. Primary learners are more comfortable working with such objects, but this technique can also work effectively with older students if the purpose is clear.

Try this ☞ **Listen and watch**

Use Lego pieces to represent the main events and actions when telling students a story, an anecdote, a joke, etc. containing new language. Give students a **gist question** to answer about the narrative and then distribute more Lego pieces equally among students. As you retell the story, they have to replicate the events and actions as closely as possible with the Lego pieces. At the end, using the appropriate representations of meaning, elicit the sentences containing the new language and write them on the board. Students can refer to this while trying to retell the story.

Try this ☞ **Listen and draw**

After introducing the topic, read out a text at normal speed containing a new grammatical structure. Ask students to draw stick figures or sketches of as many of the ideas from the text as they can, scattering them all over the page. After the first listening, students work in pairs to compare their drawings. Make sure that students do not have enough time to draw all of the ideas at the first attempt, and repeat this process several times to give them plenty of exposure to the new language.

✓ Getting it right

Challenging learners

If the text is quite challenging, let students draw during the dictation.
If the text is fairly straightforward, however, do delayed dictation, in which students are only allowed to start drawing after you have finished reading out the text.

Why this works ⟫

> **Visual representations**
>
> During the pair-check phase, students have to recall the new language and help each other work out its meaning. In this way, the pieces or drawings serve as a micro-teaching tool within the small groups. Also, the repetition of new structures and the support of the objects or pictures mean that learners are more likely to remember the structures and be able to recall them later.

Developing noticing skills

The skill of being able to notice differences, similarities, and changes is a key component of successful learning. In the mixed-ability classroom, it is important to develop learners' noticing skills, both generally and in relation to language. One way of doing this is by testing their awareness of subtle changes made to the classroom surroundings, before applying the same observation skills to the analysis of language that is in front of them. Once they become adept at noticing small changes in their immediate environment, learners are likely to become much better at it when working with new language.

Try this ☞ **Did you notice?**

Write a new word in the corner of the board, but do not draw students' attention to it. Continue teaching as normal. After a few minutes, clean the board. Then ask: *What was on the board? Can anybody remember? Did you notice?* If nobody noticed it, do not do anything with it. Next time you use this technique, students are more likely to be alert to the new word appearing and disappearing. If they did notice the word, use eliciting techniques to confirm its meaning.

Input working modes

The responsibility for presenting and clarifying new language usually falls on the teacher, who is typically the learners' principal language resource. In the mixed-ability classroom, however, it is worth seeking alternatives that reduce reliance on the teacher. By introducing cooperative working modes, where learners can make use of other available resources and support – including the knowledge of others in the group – a higher degree of responsibility can be given to learners themselves. Offering them choices can give learners a degree of control over the language they work with, and can provide them with opportunities to discover new language for themselves.

Try this ☞ **Three Bs**

Advise students to use the 'Three Bs' when working with texts containing new language.

Brain: First, tell them to look at the text carefully and underline any words they want to know the meaning of.

Buddy: Then put them into mixed pairs (one weaker learner and one stronger one) and ask them to try to work out the meaning of the underlined words together.

Book: Finally, let them turn to the reference pages of the coursebook or any other available resources.

Clarify any unanswered questions at the end.

Try this ☞ **Student teachers**

Tell your class that they will have the chance to take on the role of the teacher. Group students into pairs (for ideas how to do this, see Chapter 4) and ask them to choose either a grammar point or a set of vocabulary from the coursebook that they would like to teach. Give students Table 10.1 to complete to help them prepare for their mini lesson.

1	How are you going to introduce the topic in a fun or interesting way?
2	How are you going to show the meaning of the new word/grammar?
3	How are you going to check if the others understand the meaning of the new word/grammar?
4	Is there anything interesting that you could add?

TABLE 10.1   *Preparation for students' mini lesson*

Why this works ⫸

> **Student teachers**
>
> Students enjoy the challenge of teaching. Giving them the time and responsibility to prepare a presentation encourages autonomy. Also, thinking about how they are going to teach something is a good way of checking their own understanding. With practice, they are sometimes able to explain certain points just as effectively – or even better – than teachers, through developing their own unique content. By providing students with a chance to step into the teacher's shoes, we can also generate empathy towards one another and a greater understanding of each other's needs.

Wrestling with new language

Once learners have been presented with the new language, the next challenge for them is to begin working with it. Through setting open-ended tasks and differentiated activities, we can help learners in mixed-ability groups to put new language to authentic use in a personalized and meaningful way.

This learning stage usually takes place right after students have been presented with the language in focus, so some of the activities that follow are directly linked to the ones presented in the first part of this chapter.

Try this ☞ **Reconstructing text from Lego**

As a follow-up to 'Listen and watch' (see page 46), students work in small groups to retell the story themselves, making use of the Lego pieces to demonstrate the meaning of the new language.

Try this ☞   **Reconstructing text from drawings**

As a follow-up to 'Listen and draw' (see page 46), students work in groups to reconstruct the original text as closely as possible based on their drawings. Students can help each other fill in any missing parts by forming new groups with other students.

Try this ☞   **Mapping the words**

Give each student a copy of a simple map of the world. Read out the new words and ask students to put them on the map wherever they think they belong. Here students will need to come up with associations of their own. For example, some students might place the word 'beautiful' over France, while others might choose to place it on Japan, depending on their own experiences or assumptions.

It is important to tell students to find places for the words they don't know or are not sure about. These generally tend to be the countries they have not been to and know little about. Once they have finished writing the words on their maps, students share the locations of each word, justifying their choices. Finally, ask them to help each other with the words they did not know and make any necessary changes on the maps.

Try this ☞   **Reconstructing text**

One way of giving students controlled practice of the target language is by asking them to reconstruct a text by adding the necessary words and punctuation. Offer the right amount of support or challenge to your students by removing fewer or more words. Students first try to reconstruct the text on their own, then pair up with others who had the same version of the materials. Finally, they work together in mixed pairs.

Table 10.2 is an example about two brothers who invented the modern pen, and practises the past simple tense. Version A is more challenging for students than Version B.

Version A	Version B
no/ballpoint pens/1938	There/no/ballpoint pens/until 1938
invented/two brothers/György/László Bíró	The ballpoint pen/invented/two brothers/György and László Bíró
Hungarian/live/in/Argentina	They/Hungarian/but/live/in/Argentina
László's birthday/29th September/'Inventors' Day'/Argentina	Now László's birthday/29th September/'Inventors' Day'/Argentina

TABLE 10.2   *Two versions for text reconstruction*

11   Reading and listening

Preparing to read or listen

A pre-reading or pre-listening preparation stage is an essential component of every language lesson as an aid to understanding. In the mixed-ability classroom, however, it needs to be even more carefully planned and staged in order to assist learners of different language levels.

Two important things need to take place during the preparation stage. These can be broken down into separate pair-work or group-work phases, in which learners can share their knowledge. Firstly, learners of all levels need to be prompted to think about what they already know in connection with the topic, and to anticipate the possible content of the text. Secondly, they should be encouraged to anticipate particular words and phrases they are expecting to encounter in the text.

Try this ☞   **Reformulating L1 predictions**

Working in pairs, students predict the content based on the title of the text and its accompanying images. This can be done in L1, enabling students to express their predictions freely. Then elicit their ideas, allowing them to contribute either in English or the mother language. Put all of these ideas on the board, and with the help of stronger students reformulate into English all of the contributions made in L1.

Why this works ⫸

> **Reformulating L1 predictions**
>
> If learners are first allowed to discuss the possible content in L1, they will then find it easier to understand the text in English. Also, as a result of reformulating ideas into English, learners are given immediate access to the language that might come up in the text.

Try this ☞   **My questions**

After introducing the topic of the text, ask students to think of a few questions they would like to find the answers to, either in L1 or in English. In small groups, students think of words that might come up in relation to the answers to these questions and help each other to express them in English. For example, if the topic of the text is 'Electronic obsessions', one question students might want to ask is: *Can people become addicted to Facebook?* They could also anticipate that words/expressions such as 'spend time' and 'online' would come up as part of the answer. Students then read the text to find the information they are looking for.

Try this ☞ **Sounds of silence**

Priming students to be more attentive to the sounds around them can be an effective way to prepare them for listening activities, especially at the beginning of the lesson when students might be unfocused. Ask students to close their eyes and listen to the sounds they can hear. Make noises, for example, by dropping a pencil, walking, or drinking. Ask students to compare what they heard and speculate about what may have happened (e.g. *I think someone drank some water*).

Making tasks manageable

It is very important to make sure that the tasks we set are achievable for students with different abilities, and so we need to set personal goals for them to achieve with each task.

This can be accomplished through setting differentiated and open-ended tasks, and offering choices whenever possible.

Try this ☞ **Offering choice**

Give students the option of <u>not</u> answering all of the questions when completing comprehension-check exercises from the coursebook. Instead, let them decide which ones they would like to tackle, with the condition that they have to answer an agreed minimum number of questions, perhaps half of those listed.

Try this ☞ **How true or how false?**

Ask students to answer true/false questions on a scale of one to five, where 1 = *I am completely sure it is true* and 5 = *I am completely sure it is false*. Number 3, probably indicating they do not know, is still a valid answer as long as it can be justified, for example by saying *I'm not sure* or *It depends*.

✓*Getting it right* **Accepting all answers**

Students should be encouraged to respond creatively to the content of the text they read or listen to. Accept any answers from students as long as they can justify why they gave a certain number as an answer to a particular statement. When they justify their answers, let them use L1, then reformulate together, giving them an opportunity to say what they really want to say.

Why this works ⫸ **Open-ended activities**

Closed true/false questions do not leave students who may need more support with a lot of room for manoeuvre. The 'how true/how false' technique makes the activity open-ended and provides students with more options. It also provides the teacher with useful feedback on how well students are handling the task. By emphasizing the learning process, we can increase learners' confidence and reduce their anxiety about getting the answer wrong.

Try this ☞ **Human MP3 player**

Tell students that for the next listening task <u>you</u> will become the MP3 player!
Elicit the different control buttons of the player and draw as well as write them
on the board, as shown in Figure 11.1. Then turn your back to the class so that
students can't read your lips and start reading out the text. Students control the
MP3 player by calling out the name of the control button they wish to use. They
can stop and replay the audio as many times as they need. Students do this until
everybody has managed to complete their comprehension-check tasks.

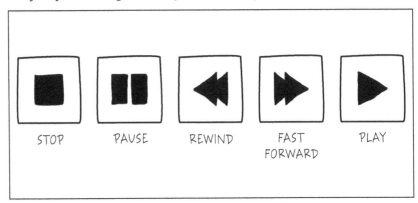

FIGURE 11.1   *Human MP3 player buttons*

✓ *Getting it right*   **Using an assistant**

You could decide to nominate a student to be the assistant who is the 'eyes
in the back of your head' and monitors for misbehaviour. Also, in case you
miss something, they could be the one to remind you. If you would like to
challenge strong students, you can choose one of them to become the MP3
player instead of you.

Try this ☞ **Using the audio script**

Let students decide whether or not they would like to read the audio script while
listening to it. Some may find it reassuring that they are allowed to look at the
audio script and will therefore automatically feel less stressed when it comes
to listening. Stronger students could be encouraged to do the listening task
without reading the audio script.

Try this ☞ **Rehearsing answers**

Before doing whole-class feedback on reading or listening tasks, first ask
students to compare their answers in pairs. Having the chance to discuss their
answers with a classmate can make students feel more confident in their
answers, and also provides them with an opportunity to ask for help.

Differentiating listening tasks

As we have seen, catering for varying language levels in the mixed-ability classroom involves making tasks manageable for all learners. In the case of listening, the easiest way to do this is to supply a range of different tasks for the same text. For example, after introducing the topic and providing plenty of preparation time, learners can be told in advance what the available options are and invited to choose one:

- **Task A:** Students listen and make note of the key points.
- **Task B:** Students listen and read the audio script in order to underline the main points.
- **Task C:** Students order the main points of a listening text from a jumbled list.

At the end of the listening activity, learners who did the same task can check their answers together. This is followed by a second pair check, in which learners who completed different tasks compare their answers. Through these mini-feedback stages, all learners will become confident in their answers.

Try this ☞ **Differentiated dictation**

Dictate a short text slowly, asking stronger students to write down as many words as they can and weaker students – for example, those who find writing too challenging – to draw the main message of each sentence on a separate piece of paper. The writers and the artists get together to reconstruct the text together. Later the sentences and drawings produced by the different students can be turned into cards for use as a memory game.

12 Speaking and writing

The key challenge of dealing with productive skills in mixed-ability groups is providing weaker students with the encouragement and help they need in order to produce the right amount of language, while at the same time ensuring that stronger students have tasks which they find engaging and motivating. The right level of support and challenge is crucial for a successful speaking or writing activity.

Providing challenge and support in speaking activities

There are a number of variables that make a speaking activity challenging, and they can be incorporated into the techniques used in the mixed-ability classroom. These variables are summarized in Table 12.1.

Variables	Effect
Familiarity with the topic	The more familiar learners are with a topic, the easier it is for them to talk about it.
Length of utterances	Longer and more complex utterances are more challenging for learners, while shorter and simple ones are easier to produce.
Planning time	Providing learners with more planning time results in greater fluency and a higher level of overall accuracy, while giving little or no planning time will result in impromptu speech.
Rehearsal time	Repeating the same task can lead to learners producing fewer errors and developing confidence in using richer and more complex language.
Non-verbal features (body language, facial expressions, intonation)	The use of non-verbal features helps the listener to understand and enables the speaker to communicate more fluently.

TABLE 12.1   *Variables involved in making speaking activities challenging*

Try this ☞   Preparing content

Help students with speaking tasks by giving them plenty of time to prepare, in L1 if necessary. Put them into mixed pairs and ask them to make note of the following:

- **Content**: what they would like to say. Both weaker and stronger students may have equally imaginative ideas.
- **English equivalents for their ideas**: encourage stronger students to help their peers come up with the right words and expressions.
- **Useful phrases to be used during the speaking activity**: both students should be writing these phrases down.

Try this ☞ **Expanding dialogues**

Give students a dialogue made up of short, simple sentences. For example:

A: Tea?

B: Yes.

A: Sugar?

B: Yes.

A: How many?

B: Two.

A: Milk?

B: No.

A: Here.

B: Thanks.

Ask students to expand each line in order to make the utterances longer and more complex. After careful monitoring and revision of the dialogues, ask students to practise the dialogue in pairs, before acting it for the class.

Try this ☞ **Rehearsal with a partner**

Get students to rehearse a dialogue with a partner by preparing their ideas and collecting appropriate language. Emphasize that this is only a rehearsal, and that students are allowed to stop or repeat certain words or chunks of language. They should also be encouraged to help each other with phrases, pronunciation, and ideas. Weaker students should be permitted to refer to their notes during the practice stage. Ask students to swap roles and rehearse the dialogue again before moving on to do the speaking activity with a new partner.

Try this ☞ **Disappearing dialogue**

Working in pairs, students practise a dialogue written on the board. They should repeat the dialogue several times, swapping roles each time. Meanwhile, the teacher gradually erases the text word by word until there is nothing on the board.

✓ *Getting it right* **Erasing words from the board**

Make sure you do not delete too many words at once. It is important to achieve a manageable challenge. Praise students for being able to fill the gaps – either with the original words or with appropriate alternatives.

Try this ☞ **One more line**

To increase the challenge for stronger students during a speaking activity, ask them to incorporate extra phrases or sentences into the dialogue as naturally as possible. These could be longer or more complex ones. Write these phrases on pieces of paper and slip them to students at random moments during the speaking activity.

Activating spoken phrases

A key feature of successful speaking is the ability to retrieve and use a range of useful phrases at short notice. Weaker students who manage to develop the capacity to recall certain appropriate phrases while speaking will benefit from a boost in confidence and a feeling of success. Stronger students need to be encouraged to use a greater variety of such phrases in order to become more sophisticated language users. Different types of repetition can be used to help students internalize key chunks of language and retrieve them when speaking.

Try this ☞ **Speed dialogues**

Think of a simple dialogue containing no more than six turns. The dialogue should contain the target phrases you would like to activate. Put students in two rows facing each other and role play the dialogues. Once they have finished, one of the rows stays still while the other moves one space to the right. Students then repeat their dialogues with their new partner.

Try this ☞ **Humming the phrase**

After drilling key spoken phrases, put students into pairs. They should have the set of phrases to be practised in front of them. Ask one student to choose a phrase and hum it to their partner, paying special attention to appropriate intonation and word stress. Their partner should try to guess which phrase it is from the list.

Try this ☞ **Use your cards**

Give students a pile of blank cards and ask them to write down key phrases to be practised during a particular speaking activity. They should write one phrase per card. Alternatively, you could give them a set of cards with pre-prepared phrases. During the speaking activity they should aim to get rid of all their cards by using them as naturally as possible.

Try this ☞ **Talk about yourself**

Give students a skeleton text with key spoken phrases to be practised. For example, *My favourite city is … I like it because …* , etc. Students fill this in with information about themselves outside the classroom, record it using the website www.vocaroo.com, and send it to you. Use these authentic audio pieces for further lesson input or as listening practice activities.

Collaboration during writing activities

The principle of providing learners with plenty of preparation time applies to writing tasks as much as it does to speaking tasks. In the mixed-ability classroom, one of the most effective ways to offer the right amount of challenge and support during the preparation stage is through collaborative working modes. Interaction of this kind not only allows learners to build their linguistic skills, it also draws on other strengths, such as the ability to select and organize ideas in a logical sequence, or being able to come up with original ideas.

Try this ☞ **Collaborative preparation**

Working in groups, students pool their ideas in L1 or in English, and also try to come up with language for each of the given categories (see Figure 12.1). After a few minutes, students circulate and give feedback on the preparation done by other groups by using smileys or question marks. They could also add new ideas or even help by translating any L1 phrases into English. Once they have seen and commented on the work of all the other groups, students return to their own plans and complete the task.

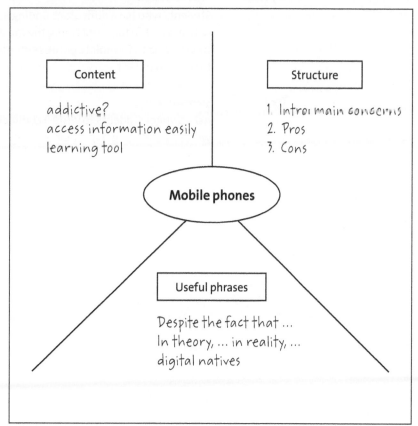

FIGURE 12.1   *Plan as preparation for collaborative activity*

Try this ☞ **Collaborative writing**

Following on from 'Collaborative preparation', groups can be asked to construct their text together. Students will need to negotiate who writes what, allocating specific responsibilities and ensuring that everyone is involved in the writing process in some way.

Try this ☞ **Digital storybook**

Put students in small groups to create a digital storybook with the help of the website www.storybird.com. They should come up with the text of the story together, but each group member is given a different role: the designer chooses the images for the story, the writer types up the text for each page of the book, and the language expert checks the language once the story is finished. The groups send the teacher and each other the link to their story to read. You can use these as input in consecutive lessons.

Individual challenge and support

It is important to create a variety of opportunities for providing learners with additional challenges or support. In particular, we should try out a variety of flexible activities that can be done individually, as there are some students who prefer working on their own.

Try this ☞ **Skeleton text**

Students who have difficulties finding appropriate language can be provided with a skeleton text containing the most important sentence starters. Rather than having to formulate entire sentences, they have to complete the text using their own content.

Try this ☞ **50-word story**

Ask stronger students to write a complete narrative using no more than 50 words, challenging both their language and organizational skills in the process.

Part 5

Getting better together

13 Focusing on the task

Defining tasks

Many of the activities we do in the classroom focus mainly on structures. Learners are asked to use or practise forms, but the only goal of the activity is for them to manipulate language successfully. If language practice activities involve little or no communication, learners will not have the opportunity to express their own ideas or opinions.

Approaches such as **task-based learning** (TBL) emphasize activities which focus much more on communicating ideas. In this context, 'tasks' have a strong goal orientation, meaning that learners need to use the language communicatively in order to achieve a meaningful outcome – which does not have to be directly connected to language.

Consider the following two activities on the topic of flags:

Activity A

After revising vocabulary for colours and basic shapes, groups of learners are each given a different flashcard showing a flag of the world, and asked to write a description of it. The collected descriptions and flashcards are jumbled up, and learners then read each other's descriptions and match each one to the correct flag.

Activity B

After revising vocabulary for colours and basic shapes, learners design a flag for their school, discussing their ideas and drawing the flag together. They write a description of their design or present it orally to the rest of the group, also describing why they have chosen each element and what it represents. Learners discuss the designs and decide which one they like the most.

Activity A is an effective way to practise the chosen vocabulary sets, and may well be engaging for learners who are interested in the topic. The matching activity is a good way to check understanding, but learners are not asked to communicate new meaning. Activity B also involves the checking and practising of vocabulary, but in addition it allows learners to work together and express their own ideas creatively. The personalized topic (*a flag for their school*) also ensures that the context of the activity is relevant and meaningful to all the learners. These added features are what make Activity B a much more effective task.

Because tasks focus on meaning and allow learners to achieve non-linguistic outcomes in addition to language practice, they are particularly suited to the mixed-ability classroom, where we need to look beyond language in order to make group-learning activities engaging and motivating for learners who have different strengths and interests.

Designing tasks for the mixed-ability classroom

Designing a task firstly involves identifying a meaningful objective that we would like the learners to achieve. We might ask ourselves: 'What is the end product of the task going to be?' The answer depends on the individuals in the group, but it might be a solution to a problem, a design for a product, or an idea for a special event. For example, if the topic is 'school', possible tasks might be linked to a relevant aspect of life in the learners' school, such as graffiti on the desks. To begin with, students could be asked to discuss why they think it happens, and whether they think it is a bad thing or not. Then the focus could turn to what can be done to deter unwanted graffiti.

At this point it is worth focusing on the strengths and interests of the group that are not connected to language learning, in order to consider how they might be harnessed productively in the task. We should ask ourselves: 'What else are these learners good at?' Depending on the group, the answers might be things such as creative thinking, art and design, or technology. So for our graffiti-related task, we might be looking for ways to get students to 'think outside the box', to design a piece of equipment, or to use a computer to create a poster for an event.

Table 13.1 shows some possible starting points for tasks related to the topic of 'preventing graffiti at school'.

Task type	Learner strengths and interests	Task objective
Solving a problem	Creative thinking	Come up with strategies to deter students from drawing graffiti on desks.
Designing a product	Art and design	Design a new graffiti-resistant desk and explain how it works.
Planning a special event	Technology	Plan an anti-graffiti fundraising event to be held at school with special guests. Create a digital poster to advertise it.

TABLE 13.1   *Starting points for tasks*

Once the idea for the task is in place and has been developed, we can begin to think about language. The task itself will determine the language that learners will need. The teacher should pre-teach language relevant to the task, bearing in mind that the primary goal of the task is to express ideas, not practise language.

Why this works ▐▶ | **Focusing on the task**

Learners' attention is on task achievement, not language practice. If the task itself is something the learners find engaging, they will be motivated to express their ideas and opinions. Because they are using language meaningfully, the anxiety that some learners associate with language activities is reduced. Collaborative tasks which enable weaker language learners to demonstrate strengths and skills not connected to language learning can also be extremely motivating.

✓ Getting it right | **Language needed for tasks**

We should make sure that the tasks we choose enable learners to use language with which they are already familiar. Important new words and concepts should be carefully pre-taught before students begin work. Bear in mind that tasks also tend to generate the need for new words; be ready to assist learners as they prepare their work, supplying new vocabulary as necessary.

Try this ☞ **My dream school**

Ask students to work in small groups to design their 'dream school'. Give them Lego pieces and explain that they will have to build a model of their school and its grounds step by step in front of the group, explaining what each part is. Allow them time to practise and rehearse beforehand, providing them with any additional language they might need.

Try this ☞ **Rock-paper-scissors tournament**

Hold a rock-paper-scissors tournament in class. As well as competitors, appoint scorekeepers and reporters. After the knockout competition, which could be filmed, get the reporters to interview the winners. Ask all students to write about the tournament, possibly in the form of a post-match report.

Adding task elements to language activities

There are occasions when we would like to put language in the foreground of an activity, and provide learners with the chance to develop their understanding in a context of controlled practice. We should bear in mind that in mixed-ability groups, activities that focus on language are more likely to be unappealing: depending on their level, learners often assume that the activity will be too challenging, or not challenging enough. One way of making these activities more engaging for learners is to introduce additional non-language goals and outcomes.

Try this ☞ **Horse/Car race**

Put learners in teams and give them some time to discuss whatever language point you have been highlighting, in order to check that they all understand. Hold a 'horse race' or 'car race' on the board using simple illustrations, in which each team moves forward one step every time a team member successfully answers a language question from the teacher.

Try this 👉 **Grammar auction**

In groups, learners read a list of sentences, some of which are grammatically incorrect. Together they decide which sentences they think are correct. Conduct an auction, in which groups use play money to bid for the items they think are correct, trying to buy as many as possible with the resources they have been given. The winners of the auction are the ones who have the most correct items after the sentences have all been checked.

Try this 👉 **Lie detector**

Ask learners to talk in pairs about what they did at the weekend, practising past tense forms. Give them the option of lying if they prefer. Whatever they say, they should try to convince their partner – the lie detector – that what they are saying is true. The lie detector listens to their partner's account, decides whether they think it is true or not, and explains why.

14 Effective study skills

Raising awareness

The gap between learners in mixed-ability groups is not only limited to how much language they know, but also applies to their knowledge of study skills techniques.

In order to help weaker learners make progress, it is first necessary to raise their awareness of what successful study involves. This is something that we can address in the classroom through activities designed to help learners develop awareness of **metacognition** – helping them to examine their own thinking. From there, we can help them identify study techniques that work for them and then create opportunities in lessons for these techniques to be practised.

There are strong links between **on-task behaviour** and successful learning outcomes. Weaker learners in mixed-ability groups can often become distracted or lose focus. They need to be given the chance to develop skills and techniques to help them concentrate and pay attention more effectively in class and while studying at home.

Learners can also benefit from the experience of others. The teacher can be an influential role model for learners; they should also be given the opportunity to learn strategies and techniques from each other.

None of those techniques can be truly effective, however, without a change in attitudes about knowledge. The classroom need not be a place for stronger learners to show off their knowledge and for weaker learners to try and hide what they feel to be their ignorance. Instead, we should be helping learners to see that 'I don't know' is actually the point where learning begins, not where it ends.

Try this ☞ **Finding out together**

Be prepared to admit that you don't know something. If a student asks you a question and you don't know the answer, be honest. Say: *I'm not sure, but let's find out together.* Then suggest ways to get the information you need or get students to suggest ways to find out.

Try this ☞ **What do you do when … ?**

Get learners to continue the prompts below and then share their strategies with each other.

1 When I read a text and I don't understand a word, I …
2 When I'm not sure about the right answer in a language exercise, I …
3 When I don't know how to spell a word correctly, I …
4 When I prepare for a test, I …

Try this ☞ **Sharing tips and tricks**

Get students to share the study techniques they use for a particular task, such as memorizing vocabulary. Give students a list of ten vocabulary items and ask them to memorize them in sequence. Then administer a quick test. Afterwards, review the scores and ask students – maybe in L1 – if they used any techniques to help memorize the items. Explain to students that people with very good memories use a variety of techniques to help them remember lists of words or numbers. Try out some of the following techniques with students and see what they think:

- placing the words in parts of an imagined building that they know well
- mentally attaching words to the faces of classmates
- creating a simple story or narrative in their mind, putting the words into the story in order.

Why this works ▮▮▶

> **Metacognitive activities**
>
> Memorizing words in a sequence is not in itself a particularly engaging task, but this activity shows that even the most boring activity can be given a creative twist. This technique gets students 'thinking about thinking' – a very important aspect of successful learning. The technique of sharing tips and tricks can also be applied to other aspects of study skills (e.g. those listed in the next section of this chapter.)

Study skills in action

In class

If learners are to develop more effective study skills, it is essential to practise in the classroom. This not only allows learners to hone their skills, it also demonstrates the benefits of having a set of conscious strategies to use. We should find time in our lessons to discuss specific aspects of study, and focus on each one separately as a mini topic. Depending on the age and level of the learners in the group, areas to focus on might include topics such as:

- identifying key passages in a text
- increasing reading speed
- effective note-taking
- recording new vocabulary
- how to check words in a dictionary
- effective online searching
- planning and drafting an essay
- how to make a study timetable

It is important not only to provide learners with practical tips and techniques, but also to give them a chance to share their ideas with each other. By activating study skills in class, we create opportunities for sharing knowledge and perspectives.

Try this ☞ **Planning together**

Set students a substantial task for homework (e.g. making a presentation, creating a poster, or writing an essay). In groups, get them to discuss what strategies they will be using. Then show them possible stages for planning a presentation/poster/essay, and get them to follow these planning stages together in class as a follow-up.

Try this ☞ **Exchanging plans**

Ask learners to write a detailed plan for an essay. Get them to exchange their completed plans with a partner, adding comments and suggestions. Learners can then amend their plans before writing the essay. As an alternative, if teenage learners say they are too tired to write a plan <u>and</u> write an essay, occasionally ask them to complete and hand in a plan only. Grade the plan according to agreed criteria.

Outside class

Learners also need to know how to make the best of their study time outside the classroom. Many of the techniques that we practise together in class can be applied when the learner is on their own, but it is also important to acknowledge that studying alone is more difficult for some learners. If learners are helped to focus on their individual needs, they can begin to develop personalized techniques and strategies for more effective individual study outside class. For example, weaker learners can be provided with suggestions for making the most of the time between lessons to consolidate their learning, while stronger learners can be guided to identify ways of setting themselves further challenges to improve their learning through self-access.

Try this ☞ **Identifying distractions**

Ask learners to identify the things that distract them when they are trying to study (e.g. checking social media, chatting with friends around them) and then get them to devise and share strategies to limit these distractions.

Try this ☞ **Commuting cards**

Get learners to write personalized study cards. Each card should contain a new word or key sentence on one side, and definitions or L1 translations on the other. These can be referred to outside class, for example while travelling to school or home as part of their daily commute. As they learn the information on a card, it is transferred to another pocket. 'Problem cards' stay in the original pocket until the information on them has been learned.

15 Dominant learners

Dealing with dominant learners

Because of the difference in personalities or in language level among members of the group, more confident learners often tend to dominate: we might see some students regularly shouting out answers, putting their hands up impatiently, talking over each other, perhaps even interrupting others. Less confident learners, on the other hand, can assume a passive role in the lesson, willingly or unwillingly allowing self-assured learners to dominate while they remain in the background.

If we are to achieve our goal of helping learners get better together, this disparity has to be tackled in some way. If we are aiming for a fairer classroom environment in which learners all receive an equal opportunity to make contributions, then less confident learners also need to be provided with the time and space to make valid contributions – and to feel confident about doing so. Simply silencing dominant learners is not the answer.

What we need to do is rechannel the behaviour of dominant learners, finding new roles for them to fulfil in the lesson without depriving them of their 'voice'. At the same time, we need to find further ways to encourage and involve weaker or less confident learners, all the time maintaining a positive classroom dynamic.

Rechannelling dominant behaviour

Dominant learners often have great contributions to make to the class and it is important that they should not feel that they are being excluded from participating. By raising awareness of the need to 'democratize' contributions and bring everyone into the picture, we can help dominant learners see that their contributions are still welcome – but that it is important to involve other learners in the discussion as well. In Chapter 6 we discussed the 'Lollipop stick' technique as a way of randomizing the process of deciding which learner to call on when eliciting responses from the class. This can be introduced as an alternative to a 'hands up' system, in which more confident learners tend to dominate.

Non-performing roles

Group tasks that contain non-performing roles can also be used as an effective way of rechannelling the contributions of dominant learners. In discussions or speaking activities, learners who normally dominate can be given roles that require them to evaluate or reflect on the contributions made by others. At the end of such activities, they can be given the chance to share their views, ideas, and opinions on what they heard.

Try this 👉 **Fishbowl discussions**

Put three or four chairs in a small circle in the middle of the room and arrange the remaining chairs in a larger circle outside, facing inwards (see Figure 15.1). Get students in the inner circle to discuss a topic, while those in the outer circle perform non-speaking roles, such as recording language, summarizing content, or taking notes of the main arguments made. Make sure that dominant learners are in the outer circle.

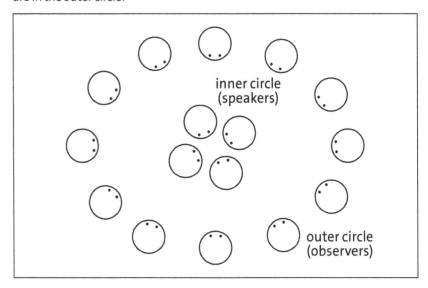

FIGURE 15.1   *Fishbowl discussion*

Maintaining a voice: mini whiteboards

Dominant learners are used to taking centre stage in lessons, and can find it frustrating if their opportunities to be heard are suddenly limited by the teacher. There is a danger that, if their voices are not heard, these learners will become demotivated and assume a more passive role. Our aim, of course, is to keep everyone involved.

Providing all students in the class with an individual mini whiteboard and marker is an excellent way of tackling the problem. By occasionally asking all students to write their answer to a question on their mini whiteboard and hold it up, the teacher is able to see and comment briefly on a range of answers, allowing dominant learners the chance to show what they know, even if they are not always called on to speak.

Try this ☞ **Five ideas I liked**

In speaking activities, help dominant learners pay more attention to the ideas and opinions of others in the class by giving them the additional task of deciding which five ideas from other people they liked the most and making a note of them on their mini whiteboard. At the end of the activity, they can briefly present their selection.

Encouraging less confident students

Removing the dominance of certain learners can potentially have a positive effect on the environment of the classroom. If stronger learners are successfully re-engaged with alternative modes of participation, weaker learners can be given more space to speak.

Shift in attitudes and behaviour

We need to do more than create time and space, however. Passive learners are unlikely to speak up until they feel secure. This requires a fundamental shift in attitudes and behaviour. In particular, we need a move away from an unhealthy 'display culture' which rewards those who already know and marginalizes those who do not know or who make **mistakes**. When learners feel that the teacher always expects them to know the answer and is asking questions merely to 'sniff out' ignorance, they are more likely to feel uncomfortable about gaps in their knowledge and adopt passive behaviour.

We need to consider <u>why</u> we ask questions in class, and what we would like learners to say about their learning. More emphasis needs to be put on what we do <u>not</u> yet know: identifying gaps in understanding and welcoming them as opportunities for real learning.

Such changes require time to get used to, and there is likely to be some frustration along the way. In order for less confident learners to blossom, however, it is vital that we remove the stigma of not knowing and establish a healthier attitude of openness, acceptance, and enquiry.

Try this ☞ **Praise for questions**

Nurture the attitude of enquiry and provide encouragement to learners by consistently praising them when they ask questions in class. Use phrases such as: *Great question! That's an excellent question. I'm really glad you asked that. Thanks so much for asking that.*

Part 6

Collaboration, creativity, and expression

16 Promoting collaboration and cooperation

Benefits of collaboration and cooperation

In traditional teaching contexts, learning is an individual activity and learners depend mostly on the teacher. This can put weaker learners at a great disadvantage: they tend to withdraw and remain in the 'background', getting little personal attention. This way they have limited opportunities to reflect on their work, and few occasions to showcase their strengths. Stronger learners tend to be in the 'foreground', receiving plenty of time and space to excel, further widening the gap between the members of the class.

Collaboration

One way to counter this tendency is to promote collaboration between learners. Collaboration draws on the strengths of all group members and engages them in the learning process. Recent research has demonstrated that collaborative tasks enable more learning to take place because learners work towards a common group goal and construct knowledge together.

One example of a collaborative task might be an interview with a teacher for the school magazine, in which one learner would be responsible for making the arrangements, another learner would ask the questions, and a third – a 'language expert' – would write it up. A further example might be a fashion show. One learner would be responsible for choosing the clothes, another learner would describe them, and a third learner would be the model.

Through roles that require less linguistic competence, weaker learners get the chance to display their strengths and have opportunities to learn from their peers at the same time. Stronger learners also benefit from collaboration, as it enables them to activate their knowledge as well as to discover areas for further improvement. Because all learners need to take individual responsibility, they become far more focused on producing a quality outcome.

Try this ☞ **Reading circle**

Show learners the website www.oxfordowl.co.uk, which contains free stories. Then put them in small groups to choose a story they would like to read for homework. Each group member has a different reading task. For example, read and write down the most interesting sentence, read and write down the five most important words, read and draw the main characters, read and draw the main scene, etc. After completing their individual tasks, children collaborate to make a presentation or a poster about the book they read to the rest of the class.

Try this ☞ **Collaborative language practice**

Put students into small groups and give them equal amounts of a certain material, such as large paper clips, building blocks, coloured pencils, pieces of string, dried spaghetti, or marshmallows. Their task is to choose a word from a set list, and to try to represent the meaning of the word using the materials at their disposal. Give them a time limit to complete their task. Once they have finished, ask other students to guess what word the other groups have built. The same can be done for sentence construction instead of words.

You could incorporate a language element by giving students a set of **functional phrases** to use during the task. Depending on the level, they might be phrases such as *Let's do …* , *Let's put this here/there*, *This is too easy/difficult*, *Why don't we put/make … ?*

Why this works ⫸

Collaborative language practice

This activity encourages students to collaborate through active communication and problem-solving. It reduces inhibitions when speaking because the focus is on task achievement rather than using correct language, and students are free to use as much or as little English as their language level and abilities allow. Some might contribute their ideas by building and being physically involved, while stronger learners might use more English to express their ideas. This creates a sense of success and achievement, and also ensures the kind of mental processes that help long-term retention of these words, regardless of ability.

✓ *Getting it right*

Collaborative learning

Initially, start with small cooperative tasks to enable students to get used to relying on each other. Give students step-by-step guidelines to help them through the learning process, and stress the fact that you expect achievement from all learners. Also, in order to facilitate the process and ensure engagement for all learners, stage collaborative tasks carefully. Use the following steps:

1   Set a group goal with a time limit.
2   Present the steps of the process.
3   Allocate roles if needed.
4   Set individual thinking time and work.
5   Ask groups to work towards the common goal.
6   Present the final outcome.
7   Give feedback on the final outcome.

Monitor group work to facilitate the collaborative process. It is also important to quickly resolve any conflicts should they arise – and make students aware of how to avoid them in the future.

When planning pair-work or group-work activities, try to provide some learners with the option of completing individual tasks. This helps to address the fact that not all students (or their parents) are going to embrace collaborative learning.

Cooperation

Collaborative processes also enable cooperation, in which learners are able to improve their individual results through getting help from others. One simple example of cooperation would be a learner who does not know the answer to a question getting a classmate to help.

In traditional settings, cooperation can still be regarded as cheating. This is a pity, as the benefits are considerable. It has a hugely positive effect on learners, changing their attitudes towards the learning process and towards their own results. Through cooperative activities they become less teacher-dependent, develop skills for autonomous learning, and are able to achieve impressive results.

Cooperation is not only a different way of working – it also changes the way we think about learning. Because it focuses on mutual improvement rather than competition between individuals, it is an ideal approach for teachers in mixed-ability contexts.

Cooperation is also a crucial part of collaborative tasks, as learners assist each other with their individual tasks. As they are dependent on the information others have, participants need to ensure that all group members complete their individual tasks appropriately. So in this section we will consider both collaborative and cooperative working modes.

Try this ☞ **Pair check**

Regularly ask students to check the answers to language activities in pairs before checking them together as a class. You can let them use L1 at this stage if necessary. Try to use pair check as a regular working mode so that it becomes natural for students to turn to each other to check their answers or to ask for help whenever they finish an exercise.

The first time you use pair check, it is important to get feedback from your students on how they feel about it. You could ask questions such as: *What did you like about pair check? How did it help you during the lesson? Is there anything you would change about it? Why/Why not?*

Necessary conditions for effective collaboration

Establishing effective patterns of collaboration takes time and patience, especially if learners are not used to working with others or have not previously had the chance to experience less teacher-directed modes of interaction. Learners need to become accustomed to the fact that they can ask for – and also provide – help when involved in group activities. One way you can achieve this is by introducing rules for helping. There are two rules to follow:
1   If you are not sure or don't know, ask a classmate for help.
2   If you do know, offer help to others.

This way, weaker learners do not feel marginalized due to lower language proficiency, while stronger ones have the opportunity to excel. Also, as learners begin to realize that their contributions are valued – and that their ideas are worth sharing – their confidence can grow together with their linguistic competence.

Try this ☞   **Trust your guide**

Put students into pairs. Ask one of them to close their eyes while their partner slowly and silently navigates them around the obstacles of the classroom, holding their shoulders and guiding them in the right direction. Play some soft music to create a relaxed atmosphere. Afterwards, encourage them both to express how it felt, before swapping roles.

✓ **Getting it right**   **Promoting trust**

Stress that it is <u>not</u> a game. Make sure students understand that they need to look after each other. Do not allow overexcited students to trick each other by deliberately leading their partner into obstacles, as this would lead to a lack of trust.

Why this works ▥▶   **Promoting trust**

The experience of looking after their partner develops empathy and a sense of responsibility. At the same time, the experience of being fully reliant on someone else builds trust among students.

17

Project work

Benefits of project work

In teaching contexts where language abilities differ greatly, it is difficult for teachers to motivate and inspire learners to do their best. This is particularly true if the work done focuses solely on language: learning words, grammar, understanding texts, using specific expressions in speaking, etc. In these cases, weaker learners do not really have the chance to get positive reinforcement regarding their language use and stronger ones are not always presented with opportunities to extend their horizons. One of the most effective ways to solve this dilemma is project work, where language is a tool rather than an end in itself.

One of the key benefits of project work is that it enables learners to pool their linguistic and non-linguistic skills to create personalized and authentic pieces of work with minimal reliance on the teacher. It allows for self-expression and produces a tangible outcome, which can take the form of presentations, videos, magazines, booklets, blog entries, podcasts, and paper or online posters. The fact that projects are completed for a specific audience motivates learners to use the language conscientiously, resulting in better outcomes and higher self-esteem.

During project work, interaction and cooperation between learners is self-directed and negotiated within groups, leading to end products that better reflect the personalities, strengths, and interests of the members of the group who created it, as discussed in Chapter 16.

Types of projects

Projects need to be used flexibly, recognizing learner preferences for different types of working modes. Some students may work best individually, while others might thrive on group work. We can cater for these needs in a variety of ways.

Projects with complementary roles

Some projects build on the different skills of the group members, each of whom has a specific task to contribute towards the final outcome. For example, if learners are asked to produce a guide to local restaurants for tourists, the roles of graphic designer, data collector, and text editor could be allocated to different students. Here, each role requires a different level of language proficiency, and the unique contribution of each individual forms a vital component of the final product. If one learner's contribution is missing, the project can't be completed.

Try this ☞ **School magazine**

The class decide together on a range of proposed content for the magazine (e.g. a crossword featuring teachers' names, an article about sports teams, a list of upcoming events, or an interview with one of the kitchen staff). The different features are then allocated to groups of students depending on the language level required for each: less challenging ones are given to weaker groups, and linguistically more demanding ones to stronger groups. In this way, learners of similar ability can be grouped together within the whole-class project.

Projects with integrated outcomes

Other projects allow for outcomes of individual work to be merged in the final product. As an example of this, consider a group project in which students give a presentation on the topic of 'What makes a good online video?' After first noting the positive features of their own favourite online videos individually, learners then present their ideas to the rest of the group and use the common points of their collected data as the basis for a group list. The advantages of this type of project are that students can work at their own pace at home first, thinking about their own criteria, which then become integrated into something bigger – the common group list.

Individual project work

Some projects can be prepared individually and then presented, either to the class during a lesson or to a particular audience, for example, to other classes. Posters prepared at home and then presented to the class are good examples of this. The poster can be either digital or paper-based. Project work of this type is an appropriate way to cater for learners who prefer not to always work in pairs and groups or who are reluctant to speak up in groups.

Try this ☞ **Science fair**

Students choose their own subcategory within the broad topic of science. They produce a presentation or an online poster individually at home for the class. Depending on the age and the level of students, topics could include unusual animals, basic experiments, scientific discoveries, or technological innovations.

Try this ☞ **Extending projects**

Following on from the 'Science fair' project, students work individually to create a crossword based on its key vocabulary. The crosswords are exchanged and completed, or they can be put aside as activities for fast finishers in subsequent lessons. Alternatively, you could ask students to create a board game in which they have to ask questions about the topic of the project.

Topics, roles, and skills

The right choice of topic for a project is crucial to its success. Learners will only really invest in a project if it is of interest and relevant to their lives. Having the option to choose the topic can be a further incentive for many learners. The subject matter can also emerge from the coursebook by further exploring a particular angle of a topic that has already been covered. For example, if there is a reading text on inventions in the coursebook, you could ask learners to come up with their own fun invention in groups (such as a machine that does homework for you!), and make a presentation about it to the class.

Alternatively, project work can be based on new topics. You might choose something suggested by areas touched on in the coursebook, or students might have their own ideas.

Try this 👉 **Group preferences**

Each group of students chooses their own topic to research to develop a sense of achievement and success. Project work produces engaging and interactive material that deserves to be shown to others. Peers, teachers, and even parents can enjoy and admire the end product of such work.

Try this 👉 **Reacting to presentations**

Students present their work and their peers make a note of questions to ask about it. Students should be encouraged to ask questions about either the content of the presentation or the process of how it was done. You could give sentence starters, such as: *I have a question about … , What/Why/How … ?* or *I really liked … in your presentation. How did you do/make it?*

✓ *Getting it right* | **Managing a project**

When planning a project, draw a mind map with the different types of language and skills that are required and prepare activities that help learners to acquire them beforehand. During project work it is important that there are no major language obstacles that hinder the process or cause frustration. Allocating specific roles at the beginning is also advisable. This often helps students focus on their task and reduces the likelihood of arguments within groups.

18   Images

Language and skills through images

The immediacy of images makes them ideal for use as input in mixed-ability classes. Students are surrounded by images: they are on the classroom walls, in the books they work from, and on their mobile devices. Images speak to us: we have a personal relationship with them. And unlike text, images do not have to be decoded; they can be accessed immediately and understood straight away.

The images in coursebooks can be exploited in free-standing activities in the classroom. One advantage of using such images is that all students enjoy easy access to a copy, and have already generated some background associations with the pictures based on the accompanying texts in the coursebook. Also, if learners are able to choose the images they work with, they are more likely to be engaged in the activity.

Try this ☞ **Photo story**

Give students a topic word (e.g. *fear*) and five vocabulary items (e.g. *door*, *telephone*, *watch*, *coat*, and *table*). In groups, get them to plan and create a photo story inspired by the topic, using all of the key words. Different students in each group are responsible for the various roles: thinking of a story, coming up with a basic storyboard, taking the photos with a mobile phone, appearing in the photos themselves, writing the captions and speech bubbles, and creating a digital photo story. (See 'Useful websites' on page 111.) Alternatively, ask students to come up with a group story using some of the photos they already have on their mobile phones.

Try this ☞ **Close-ups**

Ask students to take close-up photos of objects and locations around the school building. They share these in groups and guess what they might be. The teacher can restrict students to certain areas of the building, if necessary.

Representing meaning

Images can also be the output or end product of learner collaboration. When handled effectively, activities built around images not only ensure that all learners are involved and engaged, but also lead to enhanced learning. Images make language more memorable as they can serve as a further way of representing its meaning.

Try this ☞ **Draw and guess**

Give students pairs of sentences containing language that is easily confused, such as 'I stopped to talk to my neighbour' and 'I stopped talking to my neighbour'. They choose one of the sentences and illustrate its meaning with a simple sketch. Students exchange these sketches and identify the sentences that match them.

Try this ☞ **Jigsaw images**

Give each group of students a different descriptive text and ask them to choose what they consider to be the key words. Students create a jigsaw image made up of these words, justifying why they are using certain words in certain places. See an example image in Figure 18.1. Groups then exchange papers to use them as a basis for a discussion about their texts. Texts about famous people, such as inventors, public figures, celebrities, and athletes, are ideal for this activity.

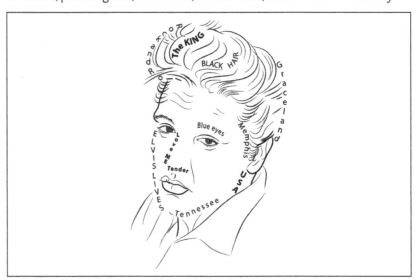

FIGURE 18.1   *Jigsaw image of Elvis Presley*

Interpreting images

Because images can be interpreted in different ways, learners of all levels can use them to create new meanings in whatever way they choose. Imagine, for example, a simple activity where learners pose questions to a figure in a painting in order to discover what that person's story might be. The teacher becomes the voice of this figure, providing made-up answers to each question asked. Information emerges as the questions are formulated, and the full identity of the figure is jointly created by learners and the teacher. By the end of the activity, learners have developed a bond with the figure in the picture, sparked by their interest in the picture and curiosity about its subject. Although the language aim here is practising question forms, the focus is on giving life to a new personality with their own unique story.

Try this ☞ **From image to dialogue**

Give students a thought-provoking image depicting several people and get them to respond to prompts, such as: *Who are they? What is the relationship between them? What is the problem?* Get students to write a dialogue between these people to illustrate the situation shown in the image. Ask students to read out their work to the rest of the class and compare their versions.

Try this ☞ **Comics**

Take copies of short comics to the classroom with the original words deleted. In groups, ask students to work out the possible situation and add appropriate sentences to the speech bubbles.

Student-created images

If we limit learners to using language, we are restricting their ability to express themselves freely. Creating images, however, allows them to articulate their thoughts and ideas, regardless of their language abilities. The meaning they convey with their images is very much personal and therefore when language eventually emerges from the picture, it already 'belongs' to the learner.

There are further benefits to using images created by students. It develops creativity and allows gifted artists to show off their skills. When learners are also the artists, their familiarity with the image and its message gives them an advantage that is missing when they have to interpret the meaning of a visual created by someone else.

Try this ☞ **Add a line**

Start drawing a line on the board and elicit ideas from students as to what it might be, accepting any answers that are offered. Continue adding lines at random, asking students to reinterpret the image that appears with each new line. As a follow-up, repeat the activity with students in small groups and get them to present their final drawings to the class.

Try this ☞ **Abstract shapes**

In groups, students draw an abstract shape on a piece of paper and speculate on what it could be (see Figure 18.2). You might provide them with useful language for the purpose (e.g. *It might be/could be/looks a bit like …*). Then they rotate their drawing through 90 degrees and reinterpret their shape from a new perspective.

FIGURE 18.2   *Abstract shape rotated through 90 degrees*

Try this ☞   **Using doodles**

Ask fast finishers or those who are tired or distracted to draw you a doodle or something specific, such as a fantasy car. Get their permission to take it to another class and show it to students. Use this drawing as the input material for a different activity with the new class, making sure that the artist is acknowledged and praised for their efforts.

Try this ☞   **Chill out and draw**

Play a piece of instrumental music, and get students to focus on the feelings that the melody evokes. Ask students to start drawing whatever it means to them. Give them a few minutes after the music has stopped to complete their work. Then ask them to share their drawings, explaining what the images are and how they are connected to the music.

Try this ☞   **Mental images**

Before asking students to write a composition about, for example, their dream holiday, take them through a visualization exercise with open-ended questions. Play some soft music and ask students to close their eyes, relax their body, and see the answers to your questions. After the visualization, students use the mental images to help them generate ideas for their composition. You could use the following script to help them visualize their holiday:

> You are going on the holiday you have always dreamt of ... Where are you going? ... You have just arrived ... Look around ... What can you see? ... Are there any people? ... If so, who are they? ... What can you hear? ... Now you start walking towards the most amazing place ... What is it? ... How do you feel? ...

19　Drama

More than words

Drama is another tool that can bring all learners to the fore in the mixed-ability classroom, regardless of their language level. Drama brings tone of voice, gestures, and movement into play, and activities that use elements of play-acting can help learners to produce language in a collaborative, original, and enjoyable way.

Students with limited language resources at their disposal can become extremely frustrated in communicative situations. By making them aware of non-verbal elements of communication, however, they can be equipped with a powerful means of self-expression. As we know, a large number of messages can be conveyed and understood through intonation, facial expressions, and body language alone, particularly when it comes to conveying feelings and attitudes. By learning how to combine verbal and non-verbal tools, learners of all levels can find effective ways to express themselves.

To begin with, we can introduce awareness-raising activities that help learners acquire some of these non-verbal techniques.

Try this ☞　**Silent film**

Students watch a short dialogue with the sound turned off. Ask them to respond to the following questions:
- Who do you think the people are?
- What do you think the relationship between them is?
- What's the situation?
- How do you know?

After discussing their guesses in groups, focus on how they were able to respond to the prompts, drawing their attention to the role of intonation, facial expressions, and body language.

Try this ☞　**Putting words in their mouths**

Following on from the 'Silent film' activity, ask students to work in groups and write a possible script for the featured scene. They could then act out their version of the scene to the class before watching the original again, this time with sound.

Try this ☞ **Ambiguous dialogues**

Give students a simple dialogue that could be interpreted in different ways. See the examples below. Each group of students interprets the meaning behind the words by responding to the prompts provided. They then act out their version to the rest of the class, using appropriate intonation, facial expressions, and body language. The audience has to guess what the situation is.

Example 1	Example 2
A: Look!	A: This one?
B: Shh.	B: Well ...
A: Look!	A: That one?
B: Shh. Not now.	B: I don't think so.
A: Oh no!	A: Why? What's wrong with it?
B: Sorry!	B: Do I really need one?

Why this works ⫸

> **Verbalizing non-verbal communication**
>
> The open-ended nature of these activities allows all learners to make a creative contribution, while the sense of achievement that results from a successful performance allows everyone to feel positive about themselves. In addition, the activities provide an opportunity to focus on effective communicative strategies.

Animating language

Once learners are aware of the different elements of spoken communication, we need to ensure that they have plenty of opportunities to put them into practice. As soon as students become aware that limited language knowledge is not necessarily an obstacle to successful communication, their confidence grows. This can have a great impact on how they deal with subsequent activities, and can substantially improve their ability to communicate successfully in other situations.

Simple drama activities which exploit non-verbal communication can be used to animate any piece of language.

Try this ☞ **In a few words**

Give students ten of some of the most frequent English words, such as: *yes, no, please, thank you, one, two, hello, bye, this,* and *that*. Ask them to work in small groups and write a short scene using only these words. The words can be repeated and reused a number of times, but no additional words can be used. Students act their scenes to the class, who try to answer the same questions as appear in the 'Silent film' activity on the previous page.

Communicating non-verbally

Depending on their cultural background, students might expect meaning to be articulated through language only, especially in the context of an English lesson. As a result, not all students feel the need to use tone of voice, facial expressions, gestures, and body language to communicate meaning. We can emphasize the potential of non-verbal communication by focusing on its expressive features when used together with language.

Try this ☞ **Mirror**

Put students into pairs facing each other. One of them starts moving slowly while their partner mirrors their movements exactly. This activity prepares students gently to use more expressive body language.

Try this ☞ **One word, one sentence**

Working in groups, students act one sentence (e.g. *Isn't this what you wanted?*) in as many different ways as possible, while the rest of the class have to interpret each situation based on how the sentence is expressed. As a slightly more challenging follow-up, they can repeat the same activity using one word only, which requires greater use of non-verbal communication.

Learning through mime

Younger learners are good at grasping meaning non-verbally. They need to experience language in a **kinaesthetic** way before they are able to express it verbally. The linking of words to gestures assists the internalization of meaning and serves as an 'anchor' for new language, enabling it to be accessed and recalled more easily.

Try this ☞ **Miming stories**

Read out a story line by line, getting students to act out the meaning of each line with appropriate movements. Try it with the whole class first, then get students to work in groups, dividing the roles between them.

✓ *Getting it right* | **Modelling non-verbal features**

Initially, teenage learners might feel silly when play-acting in front of each other. To help them overcome any inhibitions or anxiety, the teacher could be the one who demonstrates how to play around with sounds, facial expressions, and gestures. The model we provide should be exaggerated, encouraging students to laugh and helping them to feel secure. Learners might later be surprised to discover that their attempts to exaggerate voice pitch, facial expression, and body language often result in communication that looks and sounds extremely authentic.

Words 'on stage'

In mixed-ability groups, individual learner roles can be tailor-made to draw on the strengths and preferences of individuals. Learners who feel suited to their role are more likely to feel confident, while the fact that there is an audience ensures that learners will be motivated to perform to a high standard.

Finding the right role

When setting up a scene to be acted, it is important to incorporate different roles with appropriate levels of challenge. Some students will want to have plenty of lines to say, while others will prefer roles that require minimal language – or no language at all. In a performance of *Little Red Riding Hood*, for example, the lead role and the part of the wolf could be played by stronger students, while the role of grandma might suit a weaker student. Non-speaking roles, such as trees in the wood, could be reserved for those who would prefer to stay silent.

Try this ☞ **Chat show**

Set up a chat show role play where stronger students play the part of guests. To make their task more challenging, give them an unusual set phrase or expression to use during the interview (e.g. *It reminds me of what happened in Canada*). The audience will be listening out for a phrase that does not fit the context, so speakers have to be creative and 'smuggle' their phrase or expression into the interview in such a way that it goes unnoticed.

Language practice

Drama activities provide an ideal context for controlled repetition and practice of new language items in an enjoyable way. Vocabulary, functional phrases, and key grammatical structures can all be highlighted in the texts or mini scripts that we use. Repetition of key language in drama activities gives learners confidence about using it, and also enables the application of non-verbal techniques to boost the communicative value of what is said.

Try this ☞ **Charged with emotion**

Students read out a dialogue in front of the class. The teacher or other students hold up emotion cards containing words such as *irritated*, *excited*, *sleepy*, etc. at random times during the performance. When the performers see the emotion card, they have to change the way they read the next line of the dialogue. Students repeat the same dialogue several times, with different cards being used each time.

Try this ☞ **Voice-over**

Two students act out a dialogue silently, using only facial expressions and body language. Two other students watch and provide the voice-over. The speakers base their tone of voice on the manner of the actors.

Part 7   Assessment

20 Continuous assessment, self-assessment, and portfolio assessment

Limitations of traditional assessment

One of the greatest challenges facing teachers of mixed-ability classes is assessing learners. In many teaching contexts, administering the same tests to the whole class and giving them grades is a fundamental part of the educational process. Traditional grading based on uniformly administered tests can be an inefficient and potentially harmful means of evaluation, however. It hinders motivation and can develop 'learned helplessness' – the inability to overcome new situations – as well as generating a negative attitude towards learning new things. All of these factors can combine to create feelings of failure in the learner, especially for those who already have lower self-confidence. On the other hand, assessment plays a crucial role in giving learners a clear idea of where they are and in motivating them to improve further.

Due to the fact that they learn at different rates and in different ways, students in the mixed-ability classroom are best served if they are allowed to deal with tests in relation to their current stage of ability.

In order to reduce stress and anxiety, learners should be allowed to focus on the language areas of a test that they are good at first. For the same reason, they should be given the chance to tackle the test in smaller, more manageable chunks. The pressure to complete a long test in a set time can also be stressful. If learners are able to go through the test at their own pace, however, their chances of completing the tasks to the best of their ability are improved. We should also be aiming for a more flexible testing framework, providing learners with opportunities for reflection and relearning. Finally, learners should be clearly aware of the minimum requirements – and be given a reasonable chance to achieve them.

Continuous assessment

Continuous assessment incorporates all of the features described on the previous page. In the case of mixed-ability groups, one particularly appropriate continuous-assessment technique is using a **test box**.

The test box allows learners to focus on smaller and more manageable parts of language they have studied in a personalized way and gives them opportunities to reflect on their own work. It has the added advantage of providing students with the necessary space for **in-between learning**. The self-confidence of learners is boosted by being able to see the progress they are making as they go through the test step by step at their own pace.

Teachers working in settings where more traditional language-focused modes of assessment are the norm might be able to explore the potential for providing additional opportunities for assessment based on non-linguistic criteria, such as non-cognitive skills.

How to set up the test box

The end-of-unit and end-of-term tests need to be copied in multiple sets and cut up so that each exercise is on a separate piece of paper. These are placed into the test box and kept in the classroom. Learners are told in advance when there will be lessons in which some time will be devoted to test-box activities. Their task is to finish a specified amount of the tests by the end of the term, and they have the chance to do this over a period of lessons, one exercise at a time.

How to use the test box

As can be seen from the flow chart in Figure 20.1, implementing a particular sequence of activities will ensure consistency in the administration of the test box.

1 Learners choose one exercise from the test box.
2 They write their answers in their notebook, not on the paper.
3 As soon as they finish, they go up to the teacher, who marks the answers.
4 If all of the answers are correct, they get full credit for it and it is noted down in the **test grid** – see Table 20.1. The learner can then choose another exercise to do.
5 If there are mistakes, learners go back and self-correct using their books and notes; alternatively, they can decide to choose a different exercise from the test box. After the in-between learning stage, learners can have another attempt at the same exercise.

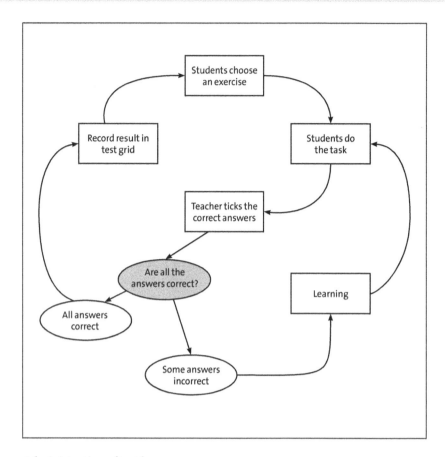

FIGURE 20.1   *Administration of test box*

The test grid is displayed in the room so that learners can follow their progress. Providing a continual reminder of how many exercises they have done so far encourages them to become more autonomous learners.

End of term 1	Exercise 1	Exercise 2	Exercise 3	Exercise 4	Exercise 5	Exercise 6
Learner 1			✓			
Learner 2		✓				
Learner 3						✓
Learner 4			✓			
etc.						

TABLE 20.1   *Example test grid*

Try this ☞   **Peer assessment**

Get stronger students and/or fast finishers to produce alternative test exercises for the test box, based on specific examples produced by the teacher as models. Exercises produced by students can be placed in a 'suggestions box', where they are reviewed by the teacher before being added to the test box proper. This can be beneficial as it enables students to consolidate their learning while at the same time supporting their classmates.

Try this    **Keeping students busy**

During other activities, direct fast finishers to the test box to avoid the frustration of having to wait for their peers.

✓ *Getting it right*   **Timing**

Make sure you plan the test-box sessions at regular intervals, for example every second week, and let students know in advance when these sessions will take place.

Self-assessment

One of the problems with traditional forms of assessment in mixed-ability groups is that it is unrealistic, like holding a running event where everyone sets off from a different spot on the track. Although it would be convenient to line everyone up neatly in the same place, the reality is that the starting point for learning is rarely, if ever, shared. Some learners already have a head start; others will find themselves well behind our chosen 'starting line'. And in each case, the distance covered and the rate of progress will depend on individual abilities.

Assessment scores tend to compound these problems further. Learners have a tendency to interpret their grades competitively, comparing their own performance to others in the group, which only leads to anxiety, hindering further improvement. In a mixed-ability classroom, therefore, self-assessment becomes crucial.

What learners have to do in self-assessment

In self-assessment, learners should:
• set personalized learning goals for themselves
• draw up action plans that suit their language level and learning preferences
• reflect on and analyse their own work
• take responsibility for evaluating their own work.

Further benefits of self-assessment

Self-assessment enables learners to take control of their own learning through setting goals and checking progress. Over time, it also enables them to compare their past and current levels of knowledge. Learners can see the extent of their improvement, sustaining their motivation to learn.

In mixed-ability groups, stronger and weaker learners benefit from self-assessment in different ways. Because it is self-directed, it makes those with lower self-esteem feel less vulnerable; and because it pushes learners to identify areas for improvement, stronger learners can become aware of their own limitations. In classrooms where everyone is striving to improve in their own way, the group dynamic also improves as learners become more accepting and inclined to support each other. Once learners have realized their own strengths, they can use them to help others.

Ultimately, all learners come to see that the 'race' is not against others but against themselves.

For these reasons if we want our students to be truly engaged in their learning, elements of self-assessment should be introduced together with traditional methods of assessment.

Try this ☞   **My personal goals worksheet**

Students take out their 'personal goals' worksheets from the beginning of the course (see page 17) to check and discuss the achievements of the goals they set for themselves.

Try this ☞   **My own test**

Students write one test question for themselves at the end of every lesson based on what they have studied. At the end of the term they could be invited to sit down with the teacher to look back at all of these questions and use them as a basis for checking and discussing their own progress.

Why this works ⫸

> **My own test**
>
> The importance of this technique lies in the fact that learning happens when the question is written, not when it is answered.

Try this ☞   **Comparing *I can* statements**

Coursebook units often contain *I can* statements for students to check their progress. At the end of the term they can go back and notice areas in which they have improved.

Try this ☞   **Reflect and predict**

Students are given a set of questions to reflect on the process of their learning, such as: *How long did you spend studying these words? Did you practise at home? Did you take notes during the lessons? Did you ask someone to help you?* Answering these questions should help them predict their results more accurately.

Try this ☞   **Traffic lights**

Use the 'Traffic lights' activity (see page 32) as a self-assessment indicator at the end of lessons. The green cup signals that they are happy with their progress, the yellow one shows that some areas still need clarification, and the red indicates that they are not happy with their progress at all. It is a useful way for the teacher to gain quick feedback on how students feel about their own work.

Portfolio assessment

In a mixed-ability classroom, it is essential that we reward non-linguistic skills as well as linguistic ones and also that we recognize the student as a whole by showing appreciation for other skills. A portfolio is a retrospective collection of different types of work – for example, posters, craftwork such as masks, puppets or origami, recordings, presentations, etc. – including the language tests done over a period of time.

By providing students with the power of choice, portfolio assessment offers both the teacher and the student flexibility, ensuring that personal strengths are highlighted in the final selection.

Implementing portfolio assessment

The first thing is to familiarize students with the concept of the portfolio and its elements. This can be done at the beginning of the year. You then need to assign a certain points value for each element of the portfolio and set minimum points targets that students need to collect in total in order to meet the requirements of the course. For example, individual elements could be awarded a points value of 5, 10, or 15 points, depending on their difficulty. Students would have to achieve a total of 100 points or more in order to satisfy the requirements. Allow students to determine how they intend to reach their points target by getting them to choose the elements they will be assessed on. Learners have to submit all elements, but can decide which ones will be assessed.

Digital portfolios work particularly well with teenagers. If the portfolio tasks are mostly done in digital format – for example, essays, PowerPoint presentations, *prezis*, podcasts, online posters, videos, etc. – they could all be uploaded onto a free digital platform, such as www.box.com. The great benefit of this is that not only can students learn from each other's work, but they can also comment on it. They can be given sentence starters to help them give each other constructive feedback. See the examples given in the 'Criteria for feedback' on page 97.

21 Grading for learning

Grading can sometimes feel like a 'necessary evil' in many teaching contexts. But there are ways in which it can be used to enable learners to identify areas for personal improvement and also to help each other to achieve the goals that they have set for themselves.

All too often learners are written off because of their errors. Learners need to see errors as opportunities for learning, not as evidence of failure. We can help them to do this by giving them a second chance to complete an exercise before grading it. In the **two-step test completion**, learning and grading take place at the same time.

Recent research emphasizes the benefits of **formative assessment**, suggesting that it can lead to a dramatic improvement in learning. **Summative assessment**, on the other hand, is a compulsory component of most educational systems, and most teachers work in settings in which they are expected to give grades. Two-step testing combines elements of both, enabling learners in mixed-ability groups to benefit from formative assessment methods while also allowing the teacher to award a summative grade at the end of the procedure.

Two-step test completion

This is a variation of the test box described in Chapter 20. The difference is that here all learners complete the same test at the same time. After the first attempt they have a learning stage before going back to take the test again, the second time focusing only on the exercises which caused them difficulties the first time round.

How to administer the test

As the flow chart in Figure 21.1 shows, the process is carefully structured to ensure that focused learning occurs between the two test phases.

1 **Attempt #1**: Learners do the test individually during the first third of the lesson.
2 **Marking**: As soon as they have finished, the teacher ticks the correct answers and leaves the rest uncorrected.
3 **Learning–teaching**: In the second third of the lesson, learners try to self-correct their test by using other resources such as the coursebook, notes, and dictionaries. They can also ask other learners for help. Learners can explain things to each other, but no writing or copying is allowed. Here, 'teaching' means explaining why something is the correct answer; 'learning' means grasping what makes the answer correct.

4 **Attempt #2:** In the final third of the lesson, learners reattempt the parts they could not do during the first testing cycle.

5 **Final marking:** As soon as students have finished, they give their paper to the teacher to have the remaining parts marked. Most – if not all – of the answers should by correct by this stage, meaning that learners get a top grade.

6 **Grading:** Based on the marks received, the teacher grades the test.

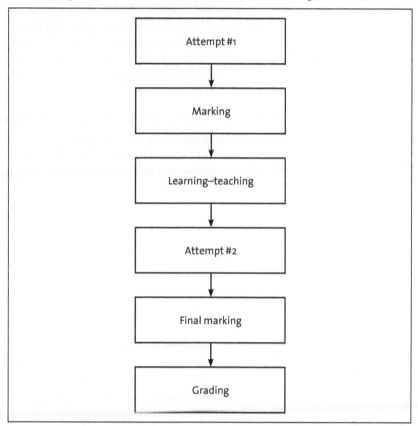

FIGURE 21.1   *Two-step test cycle*

 ***Getting it right***

Practicalities and implementation

Make sure that the activities on the test paper can be completed within a third of the lesson. Set a time limit for each step, but be flexible with learners who might need more time. Also, note that some learners might have all of their answers correct after the first testing step. They will be the ones who do most of the teaching in stage three. If you decide to implement two-step testing, do it at the beginning of the school year or term. The feeling of anxiety attached to having to do a test will diminish or disappear only if the two-step test is used on a regular basis over a longer period of time.

There might be some resistance to two-step testing in contexts where traditional assessment procedures are the norm. It is therefore important to discuss the benefits of this procedure before you implement it. Parents, colleagues, and school management all need to understand why it is being introduced and why you think all learners will benefit from it. Be ready to adapt it to your own teaching context.

Why this works ▐▐▐▶

> **Two-step testing and learning**
>
> Two-step testing gives learners who tend to underperform on tests due to assessment-related anxiety a second chance to show what they know. It also boosts the confidence of weaker learners by providing them with some extra study time. Learners who find it difficult to concentrate for long periods might underperform due to restlessness or a lack of attention. This is often the case in the primary classroom, where differences between learners' attention spans tend to be more pronounced. Providing a second chance to complete the exercises can help learners to notice their own mistakes. Two-step learning also generates authentic conditions for peer-teaching and collaborative learning.

Try this ☞   **Getting to know the two-step test approach**

Demonstrate the test cycle with one exercise, rather than doing a whole test. Get learners to share their thoughts and feelings about this approach with each other and you. You could then make appropriate adjustments to it to reflect the needs of the group.

Try this ☞   **Average percentage**

Some learners – especially teenagers – may be less motivated during the first test cycle because they know they will get a second attempt. In order to keep them fully engaged during the first test cycle, give their test a percentage score at both marking stages. Combine the two percentage scores to arrive at their final grade.

Try this ☞   **Delayed second attempt**

As an optional variation, only take students through stages one, two, and three in the lesson. Save stages four, five, and six for the next lesson. In effect, this enables learners to retake the test the following lesson with learning opportunities in-between.

Try this ☞   **Teaching partners**

Learners who have completed their tests successfully can signal to their peers that they are ready to help by using their green cups. See the 'Traffic lights' activity on page 32.

22 Providing supportive feedback

In this section we show methods and techniques that can be used to provide supportive feedback, focusing on teacher language, metalinguistic responses, criteria for providing feedback, and techniques for communicating feedback to learners in different ways.

Criteria for feedback

Students can take the next step in their learning if the feedback they receive is useful, understandable, and personalized. Grades themselves are not descriptive enough for students to see the appropriate actions they need to take. They need specific comments that show the teacher is paying attention to their efforts and trying to motivate them further. The guidelines and the sentence starters below might help you to do this.

As a general rule, it makes sense to begin feedback with something genuinely positive and constructive, even if it is not about language. For example, we could highlight a positive aspect of the student's approach to the task, such as effort or care:
- Well done for …
- The thing I like best about your … is …
- I really like the part where …

It helps to state why we like those things:
- I found … very interesting because …

We can also pinpoint areas for improvement:
- I wasn't sure why/how …
- The thing you need to focus on next is …

We should also make suggestions on how to improve:
- I think it would really help if …
- Try to …

Some students, for example those with special educational needs, may prefer to deal with and respond to smaller pieces of information at a time. For this reason, feedback should be given in manageable chunks. Teachers should identify and start with the area most in need of attention.

Language of teacher feedback

General comments

It's very easy to become frustrated with occasional underperformance of some students and use language that reveals this frustration, which makes matters worse. Consider turning negative comments into constructive questions that lead learners to solutions (see Table 22.1).

Instead of …	… say
That's wrong!	Are you sure?
	Why not go over it again?
You haven't studied enough.	What went wrong?
You haven't tried enough.	What happened?
I was expecting better from you.	How could you improve it?

TABLE 22.1   *Suggestions for constructive questions*

Praise

Praise is an extremely powerful motivational tool in the mixed-ability context, and this holds true for assessment as well. Praise that acknowledges students' effort and use of effective strategies can help sustain their motivation and self-belief in assessment situations. Table 22.2 shows key things to remember about praise.

Dos	Don'ts
• Be specific about what you praise.	• Don't patronize students.
• Praise effort as well as outcomes.	• Don't over-praise, especially when dealing with students who have low self-esteem.
• Use praise to show the connection between hard work and results.	• Don't use praise as a cover-up – challenges need to be acknowledged.
• Focus on successful and unsuccessful strategies.	• Don't praise the person, praise their work (e.g. *The paragraphs are linked logically* or *All your answers are correct*).

TABLE 22.2   *Dos and don'ts when praising students*

Try this ☞   **Tell me**

Get a clearer idea of students' efforts and strategies by occasionally asking them to explain how they did a particular task. This will help pinpoint the specific areas to be praised.

Using metalinguistic responses to elicit self-correction

The advantage of metalinguistic or non-verbal responses is that they give instant feedback to students and provide an opportunity for self-correction. It is important that we give students plenty of thinking time when eliciting self-correction. We should also remember that some learners need more thinking time than others, so it is important to be patient.

Consider codes for initiating self-correction, such as:
- pointing to a clue (e.g. a snake symbol on the board to indicate missing third-person 's', or a wall chart with irregular verbs)
- finger symbols to elicit self-correction of missing or superfluous words, problems with connected speech or word order, etc.
- facial expressions
- simple gesture (e.g. tilting your head slightly to one side).

Try this ☞ **Progress check interviews**

Conduct regular, pre-planned progress-check interviews at the end of each term in order to discuss learners' progress in a one-to-one setting. You could use *I can* statements to structure the discussion and offer further ways to improve.

Feedback on language

In order to help learners notice the way they use language and make the necessary changes, we need to provide them with helpful signals and correct versions of what they are trying to express.

Just as in the case of testing, feedback on language use should be continuous, and should focus on the type of error that learners are capable of dealing with at that stage in their learning. For example, during a speaking activity practising narrative tenses, stronger learners may need to be prompted to use the past perfect and past continuous more often, while weaker ones might need assistance with the use of the past simple. So we need to be selective in terms of <u>what</u> we give feedback on depending on <u>who</u> we give it to.

We also need to restrict the amount of feedback we give at any one time. It is important to avoid overwhelming weaker learners with a great number of errors to respond to, which only leads to frustration, confusion, and demotivation.

As well as selecting what to give feedback on, we should also try to ensure that the amount of feedback given to each learner is fairly equal. Motivation and harmony among students seem to improve when teachers distribute feedback evenly.

Try this ☞ **Desk notes**

While students are doing a speaking activity, go around and monitor language use. Write the correct versions of sentences that were used inappropriately on small pieces of paper. Give each one to the student who said it as inconspicuously as possible, for example by slipping the folded piece of paper onto their desk. It is their choice whether they look at the note and make an immediate correction or look at it later and give themselves more time to reflect.

Try this ☞   **Individualized feedback**

Record and send students individualized feedback on their writing provided in digital format using online tools. Use the sentence starters from 'Criteria for feedback' on page 97 when recording your comments. See also page 111 for free, downloadable screencasting tools.

Try this ☞   **Correct spelling**

While students are working on a particular writing activity, monitor them closely and note down all the words they misspell without interrupting them. Put the words on the board in the correct form. As soon as they have finished, they can look at the board to find the correct spellings.

Try this ☞   **Peer feedback**

Encourage students to comment on each other's work. Ask them to think of at least one thing they like about it and point out one thing they think could be improved. In case of an essay or a composition, for example, they might like the varied use of vocabulary but they might suggest linking ideas more clearly to one another. Make sure students are aware of the criteria to use when giving feedback to each other, offering separate criteria for speaking tasks and writing tasks.

Why this works ⫸

> **Collaborative processes**
>
> Generating collaborative processes allows students to learn with and from each other. The teacher monitors, guides, and provides clues, but remains in the background as much as possible. These techniques also allow students to reflect on their own work at their own pace.

Part 8

Understanding attitudes and motivation

23 Emotions, expectations, and self-esteem

This final part of the book deals with what might be going on inside the learners' hearts and heads – things that can't be easily seen or understood from the outside. This not only involves a certain amount of skill and empathy on the part of the teacher, but also a lot of noticing and reflection, which can be very difficult to manage in the middle of a hectic language lesson. Naturally, busy teachers can't be expected to find the time, energy, and capacity needed to engage with learners' inner worlds every single lesson. On the other hand, the occasions when we <u>are</u> able to show sensitivity to the factors that might be influencing our students' attitudes and motivation can result in very positive changes to the classroom dynamic. The activities offered in this part can be used flexibly, and as frequently or as rarely as you feel is appropriate for your own situation.

Impact of attitudes

Weaker learners in mixed-ability groups often fall into a negative cycle of attitudes about their abilities and become demotivated as a result. We might see learners who are dismissive about their own abilities or who are not willing to take part in the activities of the lesson, in some cases perhaps as a face-saving device – an attempt to escape situations in which they feel they might be vulnerable to ridicule. The root of this feeling is often a fear of failure based on the expectation that they will not be able to manage the tasks which are being asked of them.

A move away from negative attitudes and expectations is highly desirable. If learners are able to recognize their own negative attitudes, they become empowered to make choices about how to tackle them. With time, individual learners can begin to replace negative attitudes and expectations with something more positive.

Positive changes in individual attitudes can have a knock-on effect on the rest of the group, helping the collective learning morale to be strengthened, which benefits all of the learners in the classroom. In this way, the teacher's already difficult job of handling the mixed-ability classroom is made easier: learners who have begun to recognize and tackle their own feelings of negativity are much more likely to be cooperative and receptive to our attempts to encourage and support them in their learning. A good way to start is by tapping into the emotions of the learners in the group.

Recognizing emotional states

Rather than attempting to ignore the emotions that learners bring with them to the lesson, we can take steps to acknowledge how learners are feeling as they enter the classroom. The easiest and most effective way to do this is to ask them. The start of the lesson provides a natural opportunity to do this, while the transitions between lesson phases also provide an opportunity for 'checking in' with students' emotions. During transitions we can review how students feel about the activities they have just finished. When introducing the next task, we can do the same.

Useful questions to elicit learners' emotional states include:
- How's everyone feeling today?
- Is there anyone who's feeling nervous/bored/great?
- How did you feel about that activity?
- How are you feeling about this next task?
- Who's feeling good/not so good about it?

Why this works

> ### Recognizing emotional states
>
> This has both short-term and long-term benefits. In the short term, the responses that we get can provide us with useful information regarding our plans for that particular lesson. For example, if a large number of students say things like *We're feeling tired today*, then we might want to consider beginning the lesson in a way that is designed to help them relax and focus. In the long term, the fact that we ask learners how they are feeling can have a positive effect on their attitude towards the learning situation. A teacher who demonstrates empathy and compassion towards learners' feelings is more likely to be able to engage those learners in a discussion about learning attitudes – and is much more likely to generate the sense of security and trust that is needed for such discussions to be fruitful.

✓ Getting it right

> ### Checking emotional states
>
> It is not always necessary to pose a full question when checking emotional states. Simply asking *Happy?* or *Ready for the next task?* can achieve the same result. It is also worth bearing in mind that not all learners will feel comfortable about sharing their feelings verbally. We can acknowledge this by asking students to write down how they are feeling (e.g. on mini whiteboards) or by getting them to respond to a spoken *yes/no* prompt.

As a final point, learners actually need to be aware of their emotions before they can begin dealing with them, which is not always necessarily the case.

Try this 👉 **How I'm feeling today**

Make a poster showing a variety of faces displaying different emotions, or download and print one. For younger learners, you might choose cartoons; teenagers might prefer a poster with emoticons. Write the name of the feeling in English under each face (e.g. *relaxed*, *tired*, *confused*, *nervous*, etc.) and put the poster up on the classroom wall. Learners can refer to the emotions poster when describing how they are feeling – or point to the face that best fits their mood, perhaps learning some new vocabulary in the process.

Try this 👉 **Changing faces of the lesson**

At the end of the lesson, get students to look back and reflect privately on each activity. For each one, they should think about 'How I felt' and 'How I performed' – drawing a smiley, neutral, or sad face in each case (see Figure 23.1). Alternatively, they can evaluate the whole lesson using one face for feelings and another one for performance.

Activity	How I felt	How I performed
1	😐	😐
2	🙂	😐
3	🙂	🙂
4	🙁	🙁

FIGURE 23.1   *Student evaluation of feelings and performance in activities*

Try this 👉 **Positive gossip**

Two students in a group of three 'gossip' about the third member of the group, who turns their back and eavesdrops. Students can only say complimentary or positive things about each other.

Try this 👉 **Thumbs-up envelopes**

Prepare a set of named envelopes, one for each student. Get each student to write an anonymous 'thumbs-up' comment about a classmate – something about this person that they like. They then put the comment inside the envelope. Make sure that no one is left out by getting students to choose a name at random (e.g. by using the 'Lollipop sticks' activity on page 32).

Try this 👉 **Positive characteristics**

Working individually, students list their main <u>positive</u> characteristics under the heading 'How I see myself'. In pairs, students then list their partner's main positive characteristics under the heading 'How I see my partner'. Together they discuss and compare their lists.

Why this works ⫸

> **Supportive activities**
>
> All students in a mixed-ability group can benefit from such activities, which strengthen the group dynamic by encouraging students to support and 'champion' each other. One key benefit is that less confident students have their self-esteem boosted by hearing the positive opinions of their classmates, which can lead to an increase in motivation.

Encouraging positive expectations

If we would like to help students frame positive expectations about the learning situation, we first need to help them see the connection between their emotional state and their thinking processes. Recent research suggests that students' emotions are sometimes triggered by negative thoughts about themselves. It argues that if students have negative thoughts about themselves as learners, then this will result in negative feelings when they are in the classroom.

For example, consider a learner in a mixed-ability group who thinks: 'I got a bad score on the last test. That means I'm not good at English. I'm sure I'll do badly on the next test, too.' They will probably find themselves feeling anxious and withdrawn at the start of each lesson. This might result in uncooperative or defensive behaviour during the lesson, leading to a confrontation with the teacher or other students in the group. A negative 'thought triangle' can develop as a result.

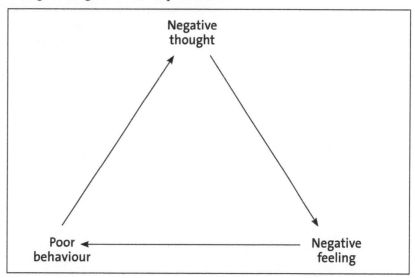

FIGURE 23.2 *Negative thought triangle*

In these situations, teachers need to be aware of two things:

- that there is something behind the student's behaviour, and
- that our own reaction to the behaviour might be interpreted by the student as further evidence that their negative beliefs are justified.

A helpful policy is to backtrack from behaviour to the feelings that are behind it, and from there to the thoughts that are behind those feelings. Our goal is to help learners see that their negative thoughts are not based on fact. And the only way to do that is to provide them with compelling evidence. The teacher's job is therefore to remain positive and supportive, and to generate situations, exchanges, and activities from which the learner is able to draw more positive conclusions.

Visualization activities

Visualization activities can help learners develop positive expectations. For example, you could read out a version of the following text to learners who have negative expectations about tests:

> Close your eyes ... Imagine you're doing the test ... You feel calm and relaxed ... You're ready to begin ... You read through the questions on the test ... It isn't easy, but you know what you have to do ... You understand ... You can concentrate ... You complete the answers ... You don't understand everything, but you can do the task ... You read through your work again ... You've finished ... You're happy with it ... You feel good about yourself!

The next step involves getting learners to imagine that it is a true story. Ask: *How were you able to do it? What steps did you take* <u>*before*</u> *the test?* By getting them to come up with three constructive steps (e.g. *I read through my notes ... I did practice exercises ... I got someone to help me prepare*), we can break the negative cycle of thoughts by showing that simple steps can lead to positive expectations and outcomes.

 *Getting it right* | **Reading visualization texts**

In visualization activities, it's important to read the text slowly, pausing for a few seconds after each sentence to give learners enough time to 'see' themselves as vividly as possible.

24

Beyond language: the whole person

Whole-person approach

So far we have suggested that the key to motivating learners in a mixed-ability group is not merely to focus on their capabilities as language learners, but also to acknowledge considerations such as their emotions and expectations about the learning situation in order to have a positive effect on their attitudes. In order for this to be successful, it is important to consider the question of <u>what</u> we teach. A whole-person approach sets targets for learning that go beyond language, appealing to non-linguistic goals such as the promotion of values and life skills. With a whole-person approach, we are interested in doing more than just getting students to manipulate language: learners are also given additional criteria for learning, such as the development of social and personal skills.

This is a great way of motivating learners in a mixed-ability group, particularly those who feel insecure about their own status as language learners. By stressing the importance of non-linguistic skills, we can create a context in which all learners are able to recognize their own individual skills and strengths. Furthermore, by recognizing their achievements in these areas, we can help them to feel validated not only as learners, but also as people.

Establishing a wider context for learning

One of the recurring challenges of teaching in mixed-ability classrooms is finding ways to establish a rapport between students and an ethos of cooperation among members of the group. If frustration among learners and friction between group members is left unchecked, it is unlikely that the activities we plan will be successful. We need to establish that values such as tolerance, acceptance, and helpfulness are not only important in their own right (i.e. in the real world), but that they are essential components of the learning environment.

It makes sense to think of the classroom as a miniature version of the world outside, in which success depends not only on gaining knowledge, but also on having social skills, values, and life skills.

Social skills

We can begin by encouraging students to identify the attitudes that are essential for successful group-work activities in the classroom, such as turn-taking, teamwork, fair play, respecting the opinions of others, and willingness to compromise. When reviewing tasks and activities, we should pay special attention to these criteria, rewarding learners not only for the language outcomes of the activity, but also the way in which these attitudes were applied. For example, we can provide extra points or good grades to groups who worked together well, in addition to the language outcomes of the activity.

Values

Agreeing on shared values is another important component of a whole-person approach. Rather than imposing values on the group, it makes sense to allow these values to emerge. Encourage students to consider values by asking questions such as: *What makes someone a good person? What are the qualities of a good group member?* By inviting them to think about these questions – first individually, and then in groups – ideas and opinions can be shared, and a group consensus can be reached. Once you and the group have identified and agreed on the values that you consider important, they become an underlying component of every task and activity that happens in the language classroom.

Life skills

A whole-person approach also seeks to make connections between success in the classroom and success in the outside world. Talking about life challenges is an excellent way to raise awareness of the importance of non-cognitive skills, such as perseverance, tenacity, and seeking advice from someone who can help. By getting students in the mixed-ability classroom to think about the everyday challenges that they have faced in real life and how they overcame them, we can help raise awareness of what life skills are, and how they can be of help in overcoming obstacles in language learning <u>and</u> in everyday interactions in the world outside school.

Try this ☞ **'Our values' poster**

Collect students' ideas about 'What makes someone a good person' and 'The qualities of a good group member' and use them as a basis for a classroom poster called 'Our values'. Refer to the poster when you talk about classroom incidents, for example: *I was really proud of Mohammed yesterday. Can anyone remember what he did? It's something on the poster ...*

Try this ☞ **Snakes poster**

For younger learners, create a snakes poster. Draw one snake for every child in the class and label each one with a student's name. Make sure the body of each snake is divided into lots of triangular sections (see Figure 24.1). Each time a student does something praiseworthy (e.g. makes a helpful comment, shows determination, etc.), tell them they can come out and colour in one section of their snake with a pen of their choice.

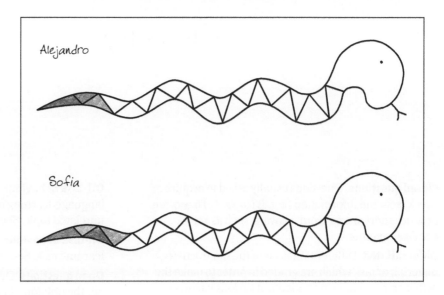

FIGURE 24.1   *Snakes poster*

Glossary

Closed questions Questions usually asked to acquire or check facts and information (e.g. *Is it open?*) They often produce short or one-word answers, such as *Yes/No*. See *Open questions*.

Differentiated Different versions of the same activity, material, or task which are graded in order to make the activity manageable for students of various language levels at the same time.

Errors Inaccuracies which show incomplete knowledge about the language; errors are developmental and usually result from incorrect ideas about how the language works.

Flow The momentum created in a lesson by a series of linked activities.

Formative assessment Monitoring student learning to provide continuous feedback that can be used by teachers to improve their teaching and by students to improve their learning. See *Summative assessment*.

Frontal teaching A way of teaching in which the teacher addresses the whole class from the front of the room; in most classroom settings, this is the standard way.

Functional phrases Phrases used to express functions, such as asking for or offering help, giving advice, suggesting, agreeing, etc.

Gist question A question that requires overall rather than detailed understanding in order to answer it.

In-between learning A learning stage where students have the opportunity to go over language points that still cause difficulties, before they attempt a test exercise again.

Kinaesthetic A way of learning through physical activities rather than reading or listening to a text.

L1 Native language; first language.

Lockstep A teaching approach in which learners work as a whole group doing the same activities at the same time, without taking into account individual differences.

Metacognition Awareness and understanding of one's thought processes about learning, for example understanding the steps involved in writing an essay: drawing up a plan, then drafting followed by evaluating and revising, etc.

Mistakes Inaccuracies which occur when knowledge about language is used incorrectly; mistakes refer to inaccuracies that students could avoid, but they might be caused by lack of attention, insufficient time, stress, etc.

Off-task behaviour Behaviour not connected to the language-learning task, such as chatting in L1 about an unrelated topic. See *On-task behaviour*.

On-task behaviour Behaviour connected to the language-learning task. See *Off-task behaviour*.

Open questions Questions often asked in order to find out the opinions, beliefs, and preferences of the person being asked (e.g. *Why do you think football is so popular?*) They tend not to produce one-word answers. See *Closed questions*.

Open-ended tasks Tasks that allow for a variety of ways of completing them, and which do not have a planned ending.

Summative assessment Evaluating student learning at the end of a teaching period by comparing it against a specific benchmark, usually by giving grades. See *Formative assessment*.

Task-based learning (TBL) An approach where students learn through communicating their ideas in order to achieve a specific task or goal.

Team learning Collaborative and cooperative ways of learning, in which students not only learn from others, but also help others to learn.

Test box A box containing the exercises from the end-of-unit and end-of-term tests cut up and copied in multiple sets with each one on a separate piece of paper.

Test grid A grid listing the names of all the students in the vertical column and the exercises of the tests horizontally, allowing the teacher to tick off the appropriate boxes when students complete a particular exercise.

Transitions Changes from one stage of teaching to the next; they can occur within a lesson phase (e.g. between activities), between phases (e.g. moving from listening to speaking) or between lessons themselves.

Two-step test completion A test completed in two steps, where students have the opportunity to revise the language they had difficulties with during the first attempt at the test, before doing the test again.

Whole-person approach A way of teaching and evaluating students that looks beyond academic ability and recognizes other factors, such as values, attitudes, and life skills.

Useful websites

Teacher training

To see the 'Mini whiteboard', 'Traffic lights', 'Lollipop sticks', and 'No hands up!' activities in practice, watch Episodes 1 and 2 of the documentary *The Classroom Experiment* on www.youtube.com

Classroom resources

Students check correct usage of words: www.oxfordlearnersdictionaries.com

Create digital photo stories: https://voicethread.com, www.pimpampum.net/en/content/bubblr, https://animoto.com

Make digital posters: www.canva.com, www.buncee.com, www.glogster.com

Find poems full of images for grammar and vocabulary input for the 'Listen and draw' activity in Chapter 10: www.poetry4kids.com

Create online portfolios: www.box.com

Students record themselves speaking: http://vocaroo.com

Students create podcasts and share them online: https://audioboom.com

Students create digital storybooks: http://storybird.com

Students create personalized online vocabulary study cards: https://quizlet.com

Find free online stories: www.oxfordowl.co.uk

Download free emoticons: www.myemoticons.com

Give personalized feedback using screencasting tools that can be downloaded for free: www.techsmith.com/jing.html

Use screencasting tools to bridge the lesson and work students do outside the classroom. See an example at: http://technology4elt.blogspot.hu/2012/04/what-is-your-today.html

Frequently asked questions

Each of the frequently asked questions refers you to specific pages of the book where you can find the answers.

Focus on learners

- How do I find out what learners are like in the class? – pp. 12–14
- How can I avoid weaker learners becoming bored or demotivated? – pp. 39–42, 72–86, 102–109
- How do I boost the confidence of weaker learners? – pp. 34–36, 76–78, 83–86, 102–106
- How can I help learners to improve their study skills? – pp. 64–66
- How can I deal with negative attitudes towards learning? – pp. 34–36, 102–106
- How can I help learners realize and appreciate their potential? – pp. 102–109
- How do I tell learners and parents that differentiation is not discriminatory? – pp. 31–33

Focus on teaching: strategies and tools

- How do I know what to teach and what to leave out? – pp. 16–18
- How can I teach in a mixed-ability classroom without increasing my workload? – pp. 19–22
- Where do I pitch the lesson? – p. 31
- How do I deal with large groups? – pp. 24–26, 72–75
- How do I group learners? – pp. 24–26
- How can I promote cooperation among learners who do not want to work together? – pp. 72–75
- How do I set up an activity when levels of competence are so different? – pp. 19–22, 60–63
- How do I introduce new language when some of the learners know it already? – pp. 46–49
- How do I get learners to work with the same reading or listening text? – pp. 50–53
- How do I differentiate without weaker learners feeling excluded? – pp. 30–32, 72–75
- How can all learners in a mixed-ability group benefit from a speaking activity? – pp. 54–56
- How do I offer the right amount of challenge to stronger learners? – pp. 27–29
- How do I get weaker learners to contribute in speaking activities? – pp. 39–43, 54–56
- How do I handle learners who become dominant because of their language competence, especially in speaking activities? – pp. 41–43, 54–56, 67–69
- How can I provide learners with constructive feedback? – pp. 97–100
- How do I get learners to do the same test? – pp. 94–96
- How do I assess learners fairly? – pp. 88–96
- How do I grade learners? – pp. 94–96
- How do I set differentiated homework? – p. 22